The Violin & A Child's Testimony

THE AZRIELI SERIES OF HOLOCAUST SURVIVOR MEMOIRS:
PUBLISHED TITLES

ENGLISH TITLES

The Violin & A Child's Testimony
Rachel and Adam Shtibel

SECOND EDITION
Copyright © 2015 The Azrieli Foundation and others

THE AZRIELI FOUNDATION
www.azrielifoundation.org

Cover and book design by Mark Goldstein
Maps by Martin Gilbert

LIBRARY AND ARCHIVES CANADA CATALOGUING IN PUBLICATION

Shtibel, Rachel, 1935–
    The violin/ Rachel Shtibel. & A child's testimony/ Adam Shtibel.

(Azrieli Series of Holocaust Survivor Memoirs)
Includes bibliographical references and index.
ISBN 978-1-897470-05-3

Also published in French under the title:
Le Violon/ Rachel Shtibel. Témoignage d'un enfant/ Adam Shtibel. Includes bibliographical references and index.

1. Shtibel, Adam, 1928–. 2. Shtibel, Rachel, 1935–. 3. Holocaust, Jewish (1939–1945) – Poland – personal narratives. 4. Jewish children in the Holocaust – Poland – Biography. 5. Holocaust survivors – Canada – Biography. Azrieli Foundation. II. Shtibel, Adam, 1928– Child's testimony. III. Title. IV. Series.

D804.196.S48 2007   940.53'180922   C2007-905438-2

PRINTED IN CANADA

The Azrieli Series of Holocaust Survivor Memoirs

Naomi Azrieli, Publisher

Jody Spiegel, Program Director
Arielle Berger, Managing Editor
Farla Klaiman, Editor
Elizabeth Lasserre, Senior Editor, French-Language Editions
Aurélien Bonin, Educational Outreach and Events Coordinator, Francophone Canada
Catherine Person, Educational Outreach and Events Coordinator, Quebec region
Elin Beaumont, Senior Educational Outreach and Events Coordinator
Tim MacKay, Digital Platform Manager
Eric Bélisle, Digital Communications and Operations Specialist
Susan Roitman, Executive Assistant and Office Manager (Toronto)
Mary Mellas, Executive Assistant and Human Resources (Montreal)

Mark Goldstein, Art Director
François Blanc, Cartographer
Bruno Paradis, Layout, French-language editions

Contents

Series Preface: In their own words...

In telling these stories, the writers have liberated themselves. For so many years we did not speak about it, even when we became free people living in a free society. Now, when at last we are writing about what happened to us in this dark period of history, knowing that our stories will be read and live on, it is possible for us to feel truly free. These unique historical documents put a face on what was lost, and allow readers to grasp the enormity of what happened to six million Jews – one story at a time.

David J. Azrieli, C.M., C.Q., M.Arch
Holocaust survivor and founder, The Azrieli Foundation

Since the end of World War II, over 30,000 Jewish Holocaust survivors have immigrated to Canada. Who they are, where they came from, what they experienced and how they built new lives for themselves and their families are important parts of our Canadian heritage. The Azrieli Foundation's Holocaust Survivor Memoirs Program was established to preserve and share the memoirs written by those who survived the twentieth-century Nazi genocide of the Jews of Europe and later made their way to Canada. The program is guided by the conviction that each survivor of the Holocaust has a remarkable story to tell, and that such stories play an important role in education about tolerance and diversity.

Millions of individual stories are lost to us forever. By preserving the stories written by survivors and making them widely available to a broad audience, the Azrieli Foundation's Holocaust Survivor Memoirs Program seeks to sustain the memory of all those who perished at the hands of hatred, abetted by indifference and apathy. The personal accounts of those who survived against all odds are as different as the people who wrote them, but all demonstrate the courage, strength, wit and luck that it took to prevail and survive in such terrible adversity. The memoirs are also moving tributes to people – strangers and friends – who risked their lives to help others, and who, through acts of kindness and decency in the darkest of moments, frequently helped the persecuted maintain faith in humanity and courage to endure. These accounts offer inspiration to all, as does the survivors' desire to share their experiences so that new generations can learn from them.

The Holocaust Survivor Memoirs Program collects, archives and publishes these distinctive records and the print editions are available free of charge to libraries, educational institutions and Holocaust-education programs across Canada. They are also available for sale to the general public at bookstores. All revenues to the Azrieli Foundation from the sales of the Azrieli Series of Holocaust Survivor Memoirs go toward the publishing and educational work of the memoirs program.

The Azrieli Foundation would like to express appreciation to the following people for their invaluable efforts in producing this book: Todd Biderman, Helen Binik, Tali Boritz, Mark Celinscak, Mark Clamen, Jordana DeBloeme, Tamarah Feder, Andrea Geddes-Poole, Valerie Hébert, Joe Hodes, Tomaz Jardim, Irena Kohn, Tatjana Lichtenstein, Carson Phillips, Henia Reinhartz, Nochem Reinhartz, Randall Schnoor, Tatyana Shestakov, and Mia Spiro.

About the Glossary

The following memoir contains a number of terms, concepts and historical references that may be unfamiliar to the reader. For information on major organizations; significant historical events and people; geographical locations; religious and cultural terms; and foreign-language words and expressions that will help give context and background to the events described in the text, please see the glossary beginning on page 223.

Introduction

When Rachel and Adam Shtibel met in 1955 in Wrocław, Poland, they felt an immediate connection. As child survivors of the Nazi Holocaust, they understood each other's experiences and comforted one another through the occasional moments of remembered pain and fear. The strength of their bond and commitment has underpinned a long-lasting friendship, love affair and marriage. During more than fifty years together, they have twice emigrated to new countries, learned new languages, built successful careers, had children and grandchildren, made friends and enjoyed travel. They pride themselves on their open communication and mutual respect.

Yet, when the couple was approached in 1996 by the Shoah Foundation for Visual History and Education to give videotaped testimony regarding their experiences during World War II, conflicting emotions were brought to the surface and arguments erupted between them.[1] As young children during the Holocaust, Rachel and Adam

---

1 The USC Shoah Foundation Institute for Visual History and Education is a non-profit organization established by Steven Spielberg in 1994. Between 1994 and 2000, the foundation recorded more than 50,000 videotaped interview testimonies of survivors of the Holocaust (which in Hebrew is called the Shoah). More information about these testimonies, as well as a catalogue of the testimonies collected, can be found online at http://www.sfi.usc.edu.

endured harrowing experiences of deprivation, fear and suffering as well as years of enforced silence that played a critical role in their very survival. In the half century between the end of the war and the invitation to give testimony, neither Rachel nor Adam wished to revisit their experiences except in rare, quiet conversations with their closest family members.

For Rachel, the call to tell her story was welcomed as a chance to explore her memories. An articulate, aware and energetic woman, she was ready to break with the silence imposed on her as a child. Adam, for his part, saw no reason to dig up painful memories after so many years of stability and success. Quiet and strong, he was nonetheless afraid of the pain that would emerge, and worried that depression might follow in its wake. After many tearful discussions, Rachel prevailed and the two were interviewed together in 1996.

The experience was a turning point for Rachel. In 1998, contrary to Adam's advice and against the backdrop of his worry, Rachel sat down to write her memoirs. It was the start of a journey of self-discovery and commemoration resulting in the beautifully written and moving memoir, *The Violin*, presented in the first section of this volume.

Adam supported his wife throughout the year she spent writing her book but, to this day, he is not sure she did the right thing. Watching her relive traumatic episodes, helping her cope with nightmares and stress-related health problems, he focused resolutely on his postwar life and still remains uncomfortable talking about his childhood. He has never been able to write anything down.

While writing *The Violin*, however, Rachel convinced Adam to locate the transcript of a testimony he gave in 1948 to the Central Jewish Historical Commission in Warsaw. From 1945 to 1948, this organization collected and preserved more than 6,000 testimonies from Holocaust survivors, most notably from children and teenagers. It was one of a handful of organizations dedicated to collecting eyewitness accounts soon after the war's end, and one of the very few to make a concerted effort to find children and take down their testimony. Adam discovered that his testimony is now housed in the archives of the Jewish Historical Institute in Warsaw, along with the accounts of thousands of other survivors. Rachel and Adam obtained a copy. Still uncomfortable with his memories, Adam was at first unable even to read the testimony as written in Polish. Rachel eventually read it, translating aloud into English as she went. This was the only way in which Adam could absorb the words he had spoken in 1948. Adam's story, entitled *A Child's Testimony*, is presented in the second section of this volume, in a translation prepared by Henia and Nochem Reinhartz in 2007.[2]

~

When World War II broke out, Rachel Chai Milbauer was four years old and living in the village of Turka, near Kołomyja in Eastern Galicia, Poland. Adam Shtibel (then Abram Sztybel) was ten years old and living in the town of Komarów, not far from Zamość, approximately 100 kilometres southeast of Lublin. Their experiences as Jewish children witnessing and surviving the horrors of the German occupation of Poland were very different. Yet, both their stories unfold against the backdrop of Hitler's racially motivated and murderous war aims.

When the Nazis marched into Poland in September 1939, they were guided by the goal of creating a new racial order in which Jews and other "inferior races" had no place at all, or were there only to

---

2 Henia Reinhartz is also the author of a memoir published in the Azrieli Series of Holocaust Survivor Memoirs entitled *Bits and Pieces* (2007). For information regarding earlier published versions of Rachel Shtibel's memoir and Adam Shtibel's testimony, see Special Acknowledgements. For more on the provenance, editing and translation of Adam Shtibel's testimony presented in this volume, see Editor's Note.

serve "racially superior" Germans.[3] The connected aims of national and ideological expansion were summed up in the goal of obtaining *lebensraum,* or "living space," in the East at the expense of Poland and the USSR, where "racially pure" Germans would settle the land and use the "racially inferior" Slav resident inhabitants as slave labour. Initial plans for the Jews in these lands called for them to be stripped of all civil and human rights, denied economic opportunities, used for slave labour, and forcibly herded into confined areas away from the general population to live under deplorable conditions where starvation and disease would lessen their numbers. In the beginning, Nazi planners thought that they might be able to "cleanse" their eastern territories of Jews through attrition, and then via forced immigration or forced confinement on giant reservations. Nazi plans for the ethnic Poles and other Slavs under their occupation called for forced labour conscriptions and massive population transfers to the East, with the aim of resettling ethnic Germans (the so-called *Volksdeutsche*) from all over Europe into newly emptied areas of Poland.

Under the terms of the Nazi-Soviet Non-aggression Treaty signed just before the outbreak of World War II, Poland was divided between Germany and the USSR. Germany occupied western and central Poland, annexing large parts of this territory to Germany proper. The Nazis also carved out a large area in the southeast of their occupied territory, where Adam Shtibel lived, as a special administrative region. The sole purpose of the *Generalgouvernement,* as it was called, was to provide a place to carry out the work of implementing Nazi ra-

---

3   While many groups were singled out as being inferior to German "Aryans" – such as Slavs and Gypsies – a special obsessive hatred was reserved for Jews in Nazi ideology. Among other things, Jews were viewed as being at the root of communism, democracy and pacifism, all of which were anathema to Hitler. In addition, the Nazis viewed the Jews as the cause of Germany's defeat in World War I, as parasites, and as the origin of all that was wrong with German and European society in the interwar period.

cial plans in the East. From 1939 onward, Jews from all over German-occupied territories were transferred to this region, as were Poles who were expelled from their homes in the annexed Polish territories further west. Decrees aimed at starving, humiliating, exploiting and isolating Jews were quickly passed and violently implemented. Adam Shtibel's matter-of-fact testimony regarding his town of Komarów, located in what the Nazis called the Lublin district of the *Generalgouvernement,* shows just how rapidly the Nazis set their plans in motion. Within days of the Nazi occupation in September 1939, stringent restrictions were placed upon Jews, property was confiscated, and all economic activity forbidden. Conscriptions for forced labour and deportations to labour camps began soon after, and by 1941 the process of detaining Jews from Komarów and the surrounding areas in a ghetto was well under way. When the Germans attacked the Soviet Union in June 1941, quickly occupying those parts of Poland annexed to the USSR in 1939, Rachel's home region of Eastern Galicia was also absorbed into the *Generalgouvernement.* She endured a similar, but greatly accelerated, process of extreme discrimination, deprivation and ghettoization in Kołomyja. Overall, more than 500,000 Jews died in ghettos and labour camps between 1939 and 1941 from disease, hunger and abuse, even before a plan for the systematic destruction of the Jews had been implemented by the Nazis.

With the invasion of the Soviet Union in June 1941, Hitler's plans entered a new and murderous phase. Early schemes aimed at massive resettlement or forced immigration of the Jews had been impossible to implement. As German troops drove deep into territory formerly controlled or annexed by the Soviet Union, the number of Jews in the areas under their occupation radically increased.[4] Nazi policies now

---

4 In 1939, approximately three million Jews lived within the Soviet Union's borders. Between September 1939 to June 1941, with the occupation and/or annexation of the eastern parts of Poland, Latvia, Lithuania, Estonia, Bessarabia and Bukovina, approximately two million more Jews lived in areas under Soviet control. In ad-

turned to the mass destruction of the Jews in the areas they occupied. In this phase of the so-called "Final Solution" to the Jewish problem, the goal was wholesale systematic mass murder. Nazi plans to accomplish this included mass shootings, the violent liquidation of the ghettos, and the deportation of Jews to camps set up for mass murder. Although they did not know it at the time, both Rachel and Adam were caught up in the implementation of these plans through Aktion Reinhard – the code name given to the operation launched in 1942 to murder all the Jews found in the *Generalgouvernement*. The Nazis methodically deported the Jews from the ghettos in the *Generalgouvernement* to the death camps at Belzec, Sobibor and Treblinka. As this process continued and intensified throughout 1942, both Rachel and Adam went into hiding in their respective areas. With luck, some quick thinking, and a few gentile friends and strangers willing to help, they managed to avoid deportation and death, thereby escaping the fate of the more than two million Jews in the *Generalgouvernement* who were killed by November 1943.

～

Adam Shtibel has only happy memories of his childhood in the small town of Komarów. Home to small numbers of Jews since at least the early eighteenth century, Komarów had a thriving Jewish community of tradesmen, peddlers and craftsmen from the middle of the nineteenth century until 1939. The available population figures for the town show that from 1856 until 1921, Jews consistently made up more than 50 per cent of the total population of the town. A religiously observant community, most Jews made their living trading with Polish farmers in the small villages surrounding the town. Although anti-

---

dition, about 250,000–300,000 Jewish refugees from German-occupied western Poland fled to the USSR after the war started. "Soviet Union," in *Encyclopedia of the Holocaust*, eds, Robert Rozett and Shmuel Spector (Jerusalem: Yad Vashem/ Jerusalem Publishing House, 2000), 415–416.

semitism was ubiquitous in this part of Poland, with restrictions of various kinds placed on Jews at different times and the occasional outburst of violence, the Jews of Komarów lived with relative stability before the outbreak of World War II.[5]

When the Nazis occupied Komarów in September 1939, anti-Jewish measures began almost immediately. Recounting the events in the spare language of a teenager focused on the facts, Adam's testimony describes increasing restrictions, harsh treatment and humiliation, his older brother's conscription into forced labour, the establishment of the ghetto and, tragically, his father's death from typhus as an epidemic swept through the confined and overcrowded space. With conditions growing worse and food becoming scarce, Adam's mother decided to send him to work as a shepherd for one of the farmers she had known and traded with before the war, believing he would be safer and better fed outside the town. This decision saved Adam's life. In the spring of 1942, as Nazi plans focused on the total genocide of the Jews, deportations and shootings became more frequent. When the Komarów ghetto was fully liquidated in November 1942, Adam was three kilometres outside the town in the farmer's village. He sat in a field listening to gunshots and screams as his mother and brother were deported to their deaths.

Following the liquidation of the ghetto, Adam found himself not only orphaned but also homeless. Farmers in the outlying villages were ordered to turn over the Jews working for them. The kind but frightened farmer for whom Adam worked did not hand him over to the authorities, but he refused to keep him on his farm, telling him that "no Jew was to be permitted to live." With no family and no place

---

5 "Komarów," in *Pinkas Hakehillot Polin* (Encyclopaedia of the Jewish Communities of Poland), ed. Abraham Wein, vol. 7, *Lublin and Kielce Districts*, (Jerusalem: Yad Vashem, 1999), 467–468. The last available figures are from 1921 when Jews were estimated to make up 60 per cent of the total population of Komarów (1,752 out of 2,895).

to go, Adam headed into the forest surrounding the town, meeting up with a group of boys and girls of similar age and circumstance. For several months, this group of children, all between the ages of eight and seventeen, wandered the countryside of the Zamość district, sleeping in forests or abandoned barns, and begging or stealing food from peasants. Adam's feelings of terror as he wandered in the forest, his profound loss, hopelessness and loneliness, come to us in a child's voice: "I wandered almost all night. I was afraid. Every movement in the forest scared me. I was not afraid of ghosts. I was afraid of people."

A series of harrowing events in the summer of 1943 led Adam to a displaced persons camp in Zamość, where he succeeded in passing himself off as a gentile Pole who had lost his parents. Adam's testimony offers a fascinating first-hand account of the upheaval, disruption and violence of the Nazis' racially motivated plans for Poland from the perspective of the Jewish child he was, and the Polish gentile he successfully purported to be. As a Jew, he experienced the deprivation and humiliation of ghetto life, witnessed the violence of the liquidation and deportations, and suffered the unpredictable mix of fearful assistance, indifference and collaboration of the local population. Pretending to be a gentile, he was caught up in the 1943 mass expulsions and forced transfers of ethnic Poles from their villages in the Zamość district aimed at "making room" for the ethnic Germans to be resettled there.

From the summer of 1943 onward, Adam's existence depended on hiding his true Jewish identity. Passing as an orphaned Polish child, and with the assistance of the Red Cross in the town of Siedlce, Adam found shelter with a young, childless Polish couple in the village of Borki. From Adam's testimony, it is clear that this couple genuinely cared for him even when they began to suspect that he was Jewish. In many ways, Adam reciprocated their feelings, but he also lived in constant fear and could never let down his guard. Dark-haired and unable to speak Polish perfectly, Adam was terrified of being found out as a Jew. His fears were magnified by the many neighbours and friends who suspected Adam was Jewish and who frequently tried to convince the couple to turn him in, reminding them of the danger for everyone if they were found to be sheltering a Jew. The couple stood by Adam and protected him throughout the war years. After the war, when Adam finally admitted he was Jewish, the couple helped him contact authorities from the Jewish community in Warsaw and assisted him in taking his first uncertain steps toward a new life.

Adam's 1948 testimony reveals his feelings toward the couple to be grateful, but mixed: they had saved him, yet he had had to hide his true identity; they cared for him even after they suspected he was Jewish, yet persistently tried to convert him to Christianity. Still, one must remember that anyone harbouring a Jew did so at his or her own peril – and those who did were few and far between. At the end of the war, Adam was one of only a handful of Jews from Komarów known to have survived.

~

Rachel Milbauer's family farm was located in the small village of Turka, outside the city of Kołomyja in Eastern Galicia. In addition to Jews, who had lived in the region since at least the sixteenth century, the area was home to Poles and Ukrainians, as well as smaller numbers of Roma, Czechs, Slovaks, Hungarians and others. Rachel's idyllic portrait of her childhood in Turka begins with evocative descriptions of her exceptionally close-knit extended family and life on the farm. Conveying the joy of the unconditional love she felt as a child, Rachel describes how her parents and family were respected by the surrounding community, both Jewish and gentile. Without commenting on whether this was the norm, she recounts many happy occasions when she played with Ukrainian friends and recalls the friendly relationships her parents developed with both Poles and Ukrainians from neighbouring farms.

Rachel's experience of inter-ethnic neighbourly relations was actually far from the norm. Indeed, relations between Jews, Poles and

Ukrainians at the local level in Eastern Galicia had a complex history of conflict and violence before the war, and these simmering tensions were exacerbated further when the area was occupied by the Soviet Union in September 1939. The twenty months of Soviet occupation brought heightened activity by the Soviet secret police and the deportation of large numbers of "dangerous elements" in the local population to Siberia, with Ukrainian nationalists as specific targets. These events sharpened the already-existing Ukrainian resentment of the Jews who were seen as pro-Soviet. When the Germans attacked Soviet territory in June 1941, they exploited this history of conflict between Ukrainians, Poles and Jews, and found many willing collaborators among the Ukrainian population. As Omer Bartov has noted, the complexity of relationships at the local level in Galicia meant that in addition to Nazi aims and policies, "the Germans had no trouble in unleashing an astonishing surge of local violence against the Jews," that made it easier to accomplish genocide and ensure its near totality.[6] The startling complicity and violent collaboration of the non-Jewish population of Galicia with their German occupiers – with Ukrainian auxiliaries often undertaking killing operations themselves – is one of the defining characteristics of the genocide that occurred in this region.

In Rachel's memoir the choices and actions of adults are played out through the eyes of a child, and it is notable that she does not address this broader background of conflict. Instead, she brings to life the sense of total bewilderment and anxiety she experienced as a young child witnessing the 1939 Soviet occupation of her town, the forced enlistment of her father into the Red Army, the German occupation in the summer of 1941, the persecution of Jews, and her moth-

---

6 Omer Bartov, "From the Holocaust in Galicia to Contemporary Genocide, Common Ground – Historical Differences," *Joseph and Rebecca Meyerhoff Annual Lecture*, December 17, 2002 (Washington, DC: United States Holocaust Memorial Museum, Center for Advanced Holocaust Studies, 2003), 6–7.

er's arrest and torture by the Gestapo (the Nazi political police). As Nazi policies unfolded in the summer and fall of 1941, Kołomyja became a central gathering and transit point for Jews from all over Galicia. Rachel and her family were forced to relocate from their village to Kołomyja in November 1941, where many of their relatives and family friends were subjected to hard labour, starvation, torture and murder – some witnessed firsthand by six-year-old Rachel.

In the fall of 1942, Rachel's parents and relatives, already weakened by daily forced labour, witnessed an increase in killings and deportations in the Kołomyja ghetto. Rumours spread that it would soon be "liquidated." The exact details of what that meant were not clear to Rachel: Would they be rounded up and shot in the town square or forest; tortured first and then shot; or taken by train to camps from which, as they had heard, no one returned? The adults in her life, however, were certain it meant death. Rachel's father decided to try to escape from the ghetto and hide as many members of his family as possible in the countryside surrounding Kołomyja, hoping they would find assistance from farmers near the family's home in Turka. Several members of the family as well as three close friends – ten people in all – managed to get out of the ghetto in the fall of 1942.

The decision to try to escape from the ghetto – and the family's ability to rely on gentiles they had known before the war – saved their lives. Soon after Rachel and her family went into hiding, deportations from Kołomyja to the death camp at Belzec began, accompanied by mass executions in the nearby Szeparowce forest. The Kołomyja ghetto was fully liquidated in February 1943.

Saved from death, Rachel and her family nonetheless endured incredible hardship, eventually finding shelter in a small underground bunker where ten people managed to survive for over a year and a half. Rachel's recounting of this harrowing period is spare and matter-of-fact. The terror and boredom of a young girl lying day-in and day-out in the three-by-three-metre bunker is apparent in the poetic cadence of her writing: "There was no room for standing and moving. When one person had to turn, all of us would have to turn. The deeper we were inside the bunker, the less air we had. [...We] were not allowed to use our voices to speak. We could only communicate by moving our lips. Turn. Whisper. Turn." Living in circumstances of almost unimaginable intimacy and dependency, the group of extended family and friends survived until the area was liberated by Soviet troops in March 1944 and they crawled out to freedom. By this time, it is estimated that of the 15,000 Jews who had lived in Kołomyja and the surrounding area in 1939, only 200 were still alive. Rachel, her family and their friends were among them.

The survival of Rachel and her extended family was in no small part due to the courage and assistance of three gentile couples – one Polish, two Ukrainian – who hid the group at different times between 1942 and 1944. Rachel's gratitude to Jozef and Rozalia Beck, Vasil and Maria Olehrecky, and Vasil and Paraska Hapiuk is profound. Her commemoration of these years is as much a tribute to them as it is to her family. This detailed record of acts of decency and kindness by these people, at the risk of death, offers an optimistic counterpoint to the more common indifference and frequent violent collaboration of the local population in Galicia during the Nazi genocide of Jews.

Rachel pays greatest tribute to her family, pointing to the enduring strength of the ties that bound them together both during the war and afterward in Poland, Israel and Canada, and holding up that bond as the critical component in their ability to survive and rebuild their lives. For Rachel's family, the decision was made to stay together no matter what the cost. On several occasions, well-meaning gentiles suggested that Rachel could pass as a non-Jew and offered to take her in. Rachel's parents refused. Yet one of the stark truths of the Holocaust is that the events and choices that led to the survival of one person could mean death for another. For many families the decision to stay together meant that all were killed, when going separate ways might have saved some, if not all. In poignant contrast to Rachel's story, Adam Shtibel survived the liquidation of the Komarów ghetto only because his mother sent him to work on the farm outside his town.

~

For Rachel and her family, the intimate bonds forged in the underground bunker in 1942 and 1943 proved strong and lasting even as they went on to face new challenges in the post-war period. Rachel's exploration of her life after the war offers the reader a rare glimpse into life in Jewish communities in Poland in the immediate post-war period as they tried to reconstitute themselves, quite literally, out of the ashes. Her difficult adjustment to "normal" life, her coming of age as a young woman, her triumphs as a musician and a scholar, her first fateful meeting with Adam, are all the more moving as it is impossible to forget the silent child in the bunker. And it is enraging, just as it must have been for Rachel and her family, to witness the shocking wave of antisemitism in Poland in the mid-1950s. Replete with government legislation and professional discrimination, for Rachel's family, the final straw came when they were faced with the requirement to change their name to something more Polish-sounding. As Rachel indignantly writes, "Our names were all we had left." The extended family, together as always, and now including Adam, left Poland for Israel in 1957 and eventually immigrated to Canada in the late sixties.

Adam, Rachel and members of Rachel's extended family thrived in Canada, and soon a second and third generation arrived. As Rachel embarked on her journey of writing and exploration, she had her daughters and granddaughters in mind. They had to know what happened. They had to understand how the family had survived. Yet, in the process of trying to make them understand, Rachel and Adam also came to see that there are no simple explanations for survival. Adam survived alone and without any of his family, while Rachel credits the fact that her family stayed together as the key to her survival. And while their experiences deepened their belief in the importance of family – with Adam coming to be loved and accepted into Rachel's family as if it were his own – some of their experiences challenge the very meaning of the word. Despite conflicted feelings, Adam's couple protected him at the risk of danger to themselves, as only parents would. Rachel hid with her mother and father in an underground bunker, but she was not protected from profound trauma, elements of which even her parents were unaware. Ending her memoir with the pre-war secrets she stumbled upon much later in her life, Rachel finally had to make peace with the fact that the family relationships she took for granted throughout her life were not what they seemed.

Adam and Rachel's stories make clear that without adult protection of some kind, children could not survive the Holocaust. Both stories also reveal that even with such protection, the trauma experienced in childhood endures. While Adam hid out in the open and Rachel hid in a dark underground bunker, both suffered an assault on their innermost identity at particularly formative ages. The defense they both employed against this assault was silence. Externally enforced in the beginning, but internally maintained afterward, this silence continued for both well into the post-war period. Freed from her bunker, nine-year-old Rachel was unable to speak, terrified that making any sound at all would mean being found and killed. She remained mute for months after her liberation. Adam made it to the end of the war convinced that he was the only Jew who had survived. After years of denying he was Jewish, it took him more than two years after the war to admit it out loud. Adam also found that he could no longer speak Yiddish, his mother tongue. He had been so afraid that he might speak it in his sleep or in an unguarded moment that he had forced himself to silence the language of his childhood, even in his mind.

Sixty years after the war, Rachel's decision to bear witness and write her memoirs is the ultimate act of breaking the silence imposed on her. While Adam's belief in the safety of silence endures, we are fortunate that he spoke out soon after the war and that there was someone there to record it. Millions of stories from the murdered Jews of Europe will never be told. By sharing their stories, Rachel and Adam Shtibel demonstrate their continued faith in humanity. We are grateful to Rachel and Adam for their courage and grace.

Naomi Azrieli
Toronto, Ontario
August 2007

SOURCES

Aly, Götz. *"Final Solution" Nazi Population Policy and the Murder of the European Jews.* New York: Oxford University Press, 1999.

Arad, Yitzhak. *Belzec, Sobibor, Treblinka: The Operation Reinhard Death Camps.* Indianapolis: Indiana University Press, 1999.

Bartov, Omer. "From the Holocaust in Galicia to Contemporary Genocide, Common Ground – Historical Differences." *Joseph and Rebecca Meyerhoff Annual Lecture.* December 17, 2002. Washington, D.C.: United States Holocaust Memorial Museum, Centre for Advanced Holocaust Studies, 2003.

Bauer, Yehuda. *A History of the Holocaust.* New York: Franklin Watts, 2001.

Bergen, Doris L. *War and Genocide: A Concise History of the Holocaust.* Toronto: Rowman & Littlefield, 2003.

Cohen, Boaz. "The Children's Voice: Postwar Collection of Testimonies from Child Survivors of the Holocaust." *Holocaust and Genocide Studies* 21, no. 1 (Spring 2007): 73–95.

Freankel, Daniel. "Nazi Ideology and Its Roots." In *Encyclopedia of the Holocaust.* Eds. Robert Rozett and Shmuel Spector. Jerusalem: Yad Vashem/Jerusalem Publishing House, 2000.

Gilbert, Martin. *The Holocaust: A History of the Jews of Europe During the Second World War.* New York: Henry Holt and Company, 1985.

Gross, Jan T. *Fear: Anti-Semitism in Poland after Auschwitz.* New York: Random House, 2006.

Hillberg, Raul. *The Destruction of European Jewry*. New Haven: Yale University Press, 2003.

Jäckel, Eberhard. *Hitler's World View: A Blueprint for Power*. Trans. Herbert Arnold. Cambridge, Mass.: Harvard University Press, 1972.

Marrus, Michael R. *The Holocaust in History*. New York: New American Library, 1989.

Rozett, Robert and Shmuel Spector, eds. *Encyclopedia of the Holocaust*. Jerusalem: Yad Vashem/Jerusalem Publishing House, 2000. Especially the following entries: "Aktion Reinhard," 103–104, "Generalgouvernement," 232–233, "Poland," 359–360, "Soviet Union," 415–416, "Ukraine," 447–448.

Pohl, Dieter. "War, Occupation, and the Holocaust in Poland." In *The Historiography of the Holocaust*. Ed. Dan Stone. New York: Palgrave, 2004.

Schoenfeld, Joachim. *Shtetl Memoirs: Jewish Life in Galicia Under the Austro-Hungarian Empire and the Reborn Poland, 1898–1939*. Jersey City: Ktav Publishing House, 1985.

Wein, Abraham ed. "Komarów." In *Pinkas Hakehillot Polin* (Encyclopaedia of the Jewish Communities of Poland). Vol. 7, *Lublin and Kielce Districts*. Jerusalem: Yad Vashem, 1999.

Weiss, Aharon. "The Destruction of European Jewry." In *Encyclopedia of the Holocaust*. Eds. Robert Rozett and Shmuel Spector. Jerusalem: Yad Vashem/Jerusalem Publishing House, 2000.

Maps

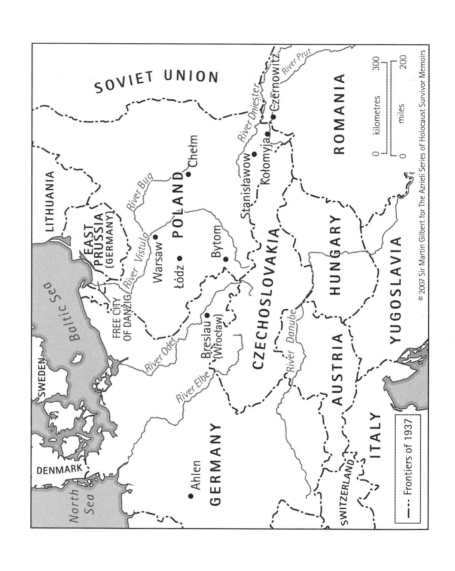

SOVIET UNION

LITHUANIA

EAST PRUSSIA (GERMANY)

FREE CITY OF DANZIG

Baltic Sea

SWEDEN

DENMARK

North Sea

River Bug

River Vistula

River Oder

River Elbe

POLAND

Warsaw
Łódź
Bytom
Chełm

Breslau (Wrocław)

GERMANY

Ahlen

CZECHOSLOVAKIA

River Danube

AUSTRIA

SWITZERLAND

ITALY

HUNGARY

YUGOSLAVIA

Stanisławow
Kołomyja
Czernowitz

River Dniester

River Prut

ROMANIA

0   300
kilometres

0   200
miles

© 2007 Sir Martin Gilbert for The Azrieli Series of Holocaust Survivor Memoirs

- - - Frontiers of 1937

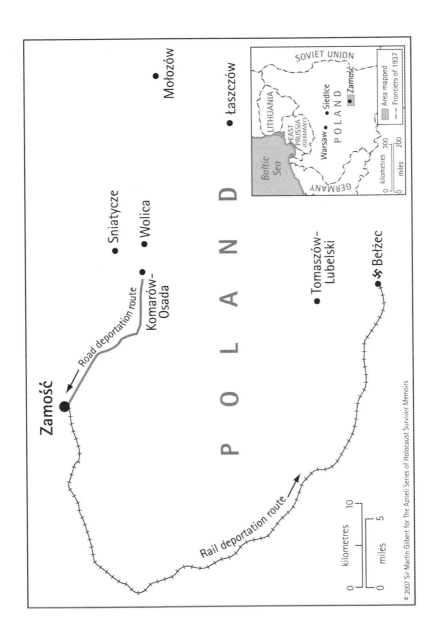

Mołozów

Łaszczów

Sniatycze

Wolica

Zamość

Komarów–
Osada

Road deportation route

P O L A N D

Tomaszów–
Lubelski

Belżec

Rail deportation route

kilometres
0   10

miles
0   5

SOVIET UNION

LITHUANIA

EAST
PRUSSIA
(GERMANY)

Baltic
Sea

GERMANY

Warsaw

Siedlce

Zamość

P O L A N D

Area mapped

Frontiers of 1937

kilometres
0   300

miles
0   200

Special Acknowledgement

An earlier version of Rachel Shtibel's *The Violin* was published in 2002 in a limited print edition and online by the Concordia University Chair in Canadian Jewish Studies (under the auspices of the Montreal Institute for Genocide Studies – Memoirs of Holocaust Survivors in Canada Program). Rachel Shtibel would like to thank Professors Mervin Butovsky and Kurt Jonassohn for the opportunity to expose her work, and for the useful feedback that ensued. All rights to the 2002 and the 2007 editions remain with the author.

A rough translation of Adam Shtibel's 1948 testimony was published under the title *Testimony of a Survivor* in 2002 in a limited print edition and online by the Concordia University Chair in Canadian Jewish Studies (under the auspices of the Montreal Institute for Genocide Studies – Memoirs of Holocaust Survivors in Canada Program). The 2002 translation was prepared by Adam and Rachel Shtibel, who added recollections and anecdotes to the English text that were not in Adam's original 1948 deposition. The translation presented in this volume under the title *A Child's Testimony* was prepared by Henia and Nochem Reinhartz in 2007. It presents only the testimony as it was originally given, with additional and contextual material offered in footnotes. For additional information on the provenance, editing and translation of Adam Shtibel's 1948 testimony, readers are directed to the Editor's Note in this volume. Adam Shtibel would like to thank Professors Mervin Butovsky and Kurt Jonassohn, as well as Henia and Nochem Reinhartz, for their work on his behalf. Adam Shtibel retains all rights to the 2002 and 2007 published editions of his testimony.

The original unedited text of Rachel Shtibel's *The Violin* and a copy of the original unedited Polish text of Adam Shtibel's 1948 testimony can be found in the Clara Thomas Archives and Special Collections of York University and are available for review by interested scholars. The original unedited Polish text of Adam Shtibel's 1948 testimony is located in the Archive of the Jewish Historical Institute in Warsaw, Poland, in Collection 301: *Testimonies of Survivors*, File No. 3683.

The Violin

To the memory of my precious grandparents, Frida and Eli Milbauer:

Dear Bubbie and Zeyde, you were the first people in my life who taught me what love and respect were. You will remain deep in my heart and memory forever.

– R.S.

Acknowledgements

I would like to thank my parents, Sara and Israel Milbauer, who were always shining examples for me. I will treasure every moment of our lives together. They truly gave me life when they saved me from the Nazis' clutches. No child could ever have been blessed with better parents. They sheltered me from what they thought would be a painful and traumatic reality until their last days. I will always be grateful to them for carefully, but persistently, keeping Velvel Milbauer's memory alive for me. And Nelly's, too. Now, after all these years, these memories have so much meaning for me. They have allowed me to see my life in a way I could never have imagined. The memory of Velvel and Nelly, and especially the legacy Velvel left me through his violin, speaks clearly to me. This was my parents' most valuable gift to me. I will treasure their memory forever.

I would like to express special thanks to my family: Joshua (Shiko) Milbauer, Moses and Mina Blaufeld, Yetta Blaufeld and Luci Zoltak, as well as to Dr. M. Nieder, for being there to save my mother's life, and to our great family friend, Baruch Ertenstreich, with whom we shared the most difficult times of our lives in the Kołomyja ghetto and the bunker in the village of Turka. I am grateful that we all survived to welcome our liberation and the renewal of our long awaited freedom. I would not be here writing this story if it were not for the heroic people who endangered their own lives to help save ours during the Holocaust. My deepest gratitude, therefore, goes to Jozef and Rozalia Beck, Vasil and Maria Olehrecky, and Vasil and Paraska Hapiuk.

I would like to thank my husband, Adam Shtibel, for whom the writing of this book was a difficult experience. I know that while I was working on this project I was not living in the present, but engrossed in the far past. Adam, I know that you were concerned about the pain and suffering I would feel if I reopened the painful memories of the past. You were right, it did open the wounds. I am grateful for your understanding and patience.

I would like to extend my warm thanks to my dear friend, Myrna Riback, who urged me to write my story. I am grateful for her help in preparing the manuscript, and her guidance and support when I needed it. I will always treasure this. I am especially grateful to Dahlia Riback for taking a special interest in my story and for her most valuable contribution in the initial editing of the manuscript.

My most heartfelt thanks go to my two daughters, Barbara Zimmerman and Iris Weinberg, for their deep devotion, assistance, constant support and advice during the preparation of this manuscript. I consider myself extremely fortunate to have such dedicated and loving children. They are my greatest treasures. I love you and am very proud of both of you. I am also thankful to my two sons-in-law, Martin Zimmerman and Dan Weinberg, for their enthusiasm and support.

Last, but not least, I want to thank my granddaughters, Shari Zimmerman, Julie Zimmerman, Ashley Zimmerman, Sophie Ostrovsky and Elisse Ostrovsky, for believing in me, for listening to my life stories, for expressing their pride and for encouraging me to write my book. I am reminded of a simple summertime breakfast in our trailer with our youngest granddaughters, Sophie, then six years old, and Elisse, then five. Neither of them wanted eggs for breakfast. Adam tried to encourage them by explaining how healthy eggs were for children. "When I was your age," he told them, "I ate eggs every day."

Elisse, without hesitation replied, "*Dziadzia* (Grandfather in Polish), how could you have eaten eggs every day? You were starving during the time of the Holocaust when you were a child and had no food at all." Adam and I were speechless. They knew us. They knew what we had been through. With this one sentence, they confirmed that we had been able to impart to our granddaughters our struggle for survival. We both realized at that moment that we had achieved our goal. The dark days of suffering and devastation under the Nazis will never be forgotten or passed over unnoticed.

Prologue

As I write this, it is the year 2000. The new millennium ushered in my sixty-fifth birthday. My life moves in front of me like coloured fragments in a kaleidoscope. I am taking stock of all that has happened and the burdens I still carry within me. It all began with my grandparents, Frida and Eli Milbauer, who wrapped me in their unconditional love, respect and devotion. They taught me the meaning of a close and caring family. In their love, I felt secure and developed a sense of self. All of their values live in me and I hope I have passed them on to my own family. I can see the continuity of what my grandparents gave me moving through the generations to my grandchildren. I treasure my own meaningful family relationships, which have only grown and strengthened through happy and sad times. I see clearly how our childhood years leave an indelible impression on our adult lives. I now realize how our Gypsy (Roma) neighbours in Turka influenced and enriched my life. Many of my pleasures and pastimes as an adult were influenced by my love of their music, their joyful dancing and colourful costumes. Nothing feels better to me than sitting around a campfire, all of my family with me, as we sing our favourite songs.

Of course the war has left deep scars. My happy childhood, my home, my loved ones are all gone. The impact of these events can never be erased. One of the saddest and lasting effects of the war on me has been, strangely, my reaction to the beautiful image and meaning of the Star of David. Being in the ghetto and witnessing how the Nazis forced the Jews to wear the star as the identifying mark that they deserved to be murdered, has made me shy away from this symbol. When we escaped from the ghetto and ripped the armbands emblazoned with the star from our arms, I swore I would never wear this symbol again. I could not even bring myself to allow my children and grandchildren to wear what should be a wonderful and proud symbol of their Jewishness. For so many Jews, the star is the essence of who they are as a people. But not for me.

VIGNETTES

Small pieces of memory running frantically
Like butterflies in a field.
I am caught as they dance around my body
Flapping wings and colours so wild
I am tempted to try and keep them
Just for me.
What I knew as truth
I now know was not.
The space between waking and dreaming is fragile.
No one ever told me
No one ever told me that it was her
That my mother's name was Nelly.

Part One:
My Life Was Blessed

Chapter 1

As she prepared her things to bake bread, my grandmother, Bubbie Frida, would call out to me, "Rachel, please come here, I need your help. You know you make the best challah."[1] Excitedly, I would run to her, calling out, "Bubbie, I'm coming. Please wait for me."

She had ordered little baking forms of different shapes from the tinsmith that were only for my use. She would give me a piece of dough and I would put them into my little tins so that my bread would come out in all shapes. She would serve my little baked goods along with her own breads at the dinner table and praise my abilities. Smiling, she would say, "It was Rachel who baked this. See how great it tastes." Then my grandfather, Zeyde Eli, would make the blessing over the challah and divide it into small pieces for everyone. As each member of my family took a bite they would call out, "Rachel, are you sure you baked this? It is so delicious." I could hardly wait for next week to come so we could do it again.

My family's farm was in the village of Turka, fourteen kilome-

---

1 A challah is a type of bread traditionally eaten on Shabbat, the Jewish Sabbath. For further explanation of this and the other Hebrew, Yiddish or Polish words used in this volume, see the glossary.

tres from the city of Kołomyja in the southeastern section of Poland, called Galicia. Kołomyja is located near the Carpathian Mountains. It hugs the banks of the Prut River and was – and still is – surrounded by villages and vacation resorts. The fresh air and picturesque location made it ideal for picnics on the banks of the river. The sound of young vacationers, their laughter and song, rang through the air when I was a child and often lulled me to sleep. Our farm was large, with many acres of corn and tobacco, grain, potatoes, sunflower and poppy seeds. When the poppy seeds were dry and ready to crack, I would crush the seeds in my palms and eat them out of my hand. I would braid the corn silk and pretend that it was hair; it was soft and golden in my small hands.

Turka was a farming community, and home to Poles, Ukrainians and close to thirty Jewish families. Everyone worked their own land, but when needed, helped one another. There was a church and a synagogue.

My grandmother, Frida, was tall and slender. She had curly blond hair, which she kept covered with a scarf. Her beautiful face was round, with a small straight nose and big blue eyes. On the large, busy farm, she had most of the responsibilities. She took care of the animals – cows, goats, chickens, ducks, turkeys and work horses. She had a reputation among the surrounding farmers as a healer, and they would often call on her for help with their animals. If a chicken had problems laying an egg, Frida would make a small incision for the egg to pass through, which she would later stitch up. When a horse was in labour, she would help deliver the new colt. Nothing was too difficult for her and although we had hired help, she enjoyed working and took pride in her farm. She would make compotes and syrups with the gooseberries, currants, raspberries and many varieties of tea roses that grew behind the house. I can still taste the syrups she made, which we drank with cold water in summer or in hot tea when the weather turned cold.

There was also an orchard with eighty fruit trees – a spectacular sight, particularly in the springtime when the trees were in full, fragrant blossom. Near the front of our property there was a deep-water well. Two pails hung from a chain at the well. When the handle was turned, one pail went down empty and the other pail came up, full of water. When I was little, I was fascinated by the well and with my own reflection in it. When no one was around to see me I would hold on to the ledge with my hands and look down into the water to see myself.

Our house was a simple, wooden structure with a straw roof. At the entrance of the house there was a small hallway where Bobby, our pet German Shepherd, loved to sleep on rainy and cold days. To the right of the entrance hall was a big room that functioned as our kitchen, dining, living, entertaining and sleeping room. Everything happened in that room. The house was always full of family, friends and neighbours who gathered in the evenings to talk and sing.

The living room faced the front of the property and had two huge windows. Under one window, there was a long wooden bench. In front of the bench was our large wooden dining table with two drawers – one for dairy cutlery and one for meat cutlery, in keeping with kosher dietary laws. Eight wooden chairs surrounded the table, each belonging to a particular family member. On weekdays, everyone ate at different times and my grandmother would cook everyone their favourite dishes. I particularly remember my uncle Velvel sitting at the table at dinner time with his newspaper spread out in front of him, often forgetting to eat his food.

On Friday evenings, Shabbat, and holidays the family gathered and ate together. My grandmother would do her baking on Thursdays to get ready. I can still hear the sounds of everyone sitting together at the table, talking, joking and singing beautiful Yiddish songs.

My grandfather, Eli, bought our farm just before his marriage to my grandmother, Frida Bajzer, and it was there that their three sons were born. My father, Israel, the eldest, was born in 1907. His brother Wolf, whom we called Velvel, was born three years later, and Joshua, the youngest, whom we called Shiko, was born in 1912. My grandfather was of medium build and had dark brown hair, a long beard and a moustache. As an Orthodox Jew, he always wore a long black coat, black pants and a white shirt and covered his head with a hat. Most days he spent sitting at the table studying the Torah. Even though he owned a large farm and loved woodworking, his greatest pleasure was studying the Torah – where he believed all wisdom began.

Zeyde Eli was a *cohen*.[2] He was very proud of this lineage and felt that he had certain obligations to the congregation and to the Jewish community. He pronounced special benedictions on religious holidays, carried out symbolic redemptions of the firstborn sons on the thirty-first day after birth called Pidyon HaBen, and received precedence at religious functions, such as the reading of the Torah.

He was known in the village as a scholar and people often turned to him, having great respect for his opinion and advice. I remember him best as a warm and soft-spoken man. I never heard a cross word spoken between him and my grandmother. I can see him now as he looked when he took a break from his reading and rested. Sitting back in his chair, he would light up his pipe and smoke – lost in thought. Once in a while, he would call me to study with him. I would rush to sit on his lap, eagerly awaiting his words. He loved to teach me the Hebrew alphabet and when I was three years old I had mastered all the letters. When anyone came into the room he would call out, "Please, come here and listen to how beautifully Chai Rachel is reading Hebrew letters."

Happily and with pride, I would recite them, knowing I was pleasing my zeyde. I knew that after my lesson he would let me sit on his lap and braid his beard.

~

2   A *cohen* is a descendant of the priestly family of the biblical Aaron, brother of Moses. In Judaism, this inherited designation is considered a great honour. For further explanation, see the glossary.

Uncle Shiko, my father's youngest brother, had beautiful, thick, brown wavy hair and wore it combed away from his forehead. His face was oval and he had soft, warm brown eyes. Shiko did not enjoy farming, so he opened a small store in the village where he sold household items such as matches, flour, candles and thread. Every morning he pinned his wide pant legs so they would not get caught in the wheel of his bicycle, and away he would go to open his store located at the other end of the village.

Uncle Velvel was my favourite, and I was his. He took me for strolls and proudly showed me off to the village. He always brought me gifts. Most of all, I loved the clothes he bought for me. He would tell me, "Rachel, I will always take care of you and buy you nice clothes, even when you are a grown up lady." I would hug him with all of my strength and say, "Uncle Velvel, I love you the most."

Velvel often took out his precious violin and played a melody for me. He let me hold the bow and move it over the strings while he played the melody with his fingers. "Little Rachel," he would say, "when you get a little older I will teach you to play the violin and one day this violin will be yours. How proud I will be of you when I listen to your music, just like you are listening to my music now." Velvel, like his brothers, was slim and of medium height. He had an oval face, with big, warm brown eyes, and a dimple in his chin. Like Shiko, he also wore his thick, black wavy hair combed up away from his forehead. He had been playing the violin since the age of ten and had a wonderful, strong singing voice. Velvel would often play at weddings and other occasions in Turka and the surrounding villages.

Velvel also had an interest in weaving kilim rugs. These beautiful rugs were made of wool he spun and dyed himself in shades of black, green, red, white and rust. After the wool was dry, he wove it on a special rug-weaving machine that allowed him to design his own patterns. The kilim rugs he created were reversible and made in different sizes, so they could be hung on the wall for decoration or used as bed and table covers. When he finished a project, he liked to show it to my mother and ask her opinion. He felt she had great taste in colour and design. My grandmother was very proud of Velvel and helped him spin the wool on the spinning wheel. As they worked together she often smiled and said, "Oh, my Velvel is so talented. Look what a great job he is doing."

Velvel became quite well known for these rugs and his interest soon turned into his occupation. He often travelled to Warsaw, where his work was in great demand, and so he rented a room there for himself and established a second home. In Warsaw, he met and fell in love with a girl named Nelly. She was very beautiful and had long, dark blond braids, a petite figure and very delicate features. I have only seen her in a photograph.

~

I slept with my grandmother in her double bed. The bed stood at one end of the large room, near the big brick wood-burning stove in the corner, which also had an oven for baking bread. There was a small window above her bed that overlooked the yard. When it rained and I was forced to stay inside, my favourite spot to sit was on Bubbie's bed. I would look out through the small window and watch the raindrops run off the deep red petals of the peonies.

It was my grandmother's job to keep the house clean and orderly. Taking care of the house was not an easy task. The straw mattresses regularly needed filling and it was my grandmother who added straw to maintain them. The clay floor had to be swept several times a day. I can still remember my grandmother sprinkling the floor with water to keep the dust down before sweeping – the tin pail and cup she used for this purpose were always ready at the entrance of the big room. The laundry was done in the stream and it, too, was my grandmother's job. I would often go with her and watch as she soaped the clothes and knocked them against large stones on the side of the shore, rinsing each item in the crystal clear water.

Of the three brothers, my father was the only one who loved to farm. He planted and maintained the orchard, growing extraordinary apples, pears (Uncle Shiko's favourite) and sour cherries (my mother's favourite). However, his special project was beekeeping, and the abundant honey from his beehives was enjoyed by our family and sold in the area. My father took care of the beehives by himself. No one else in the family would go near the bees, but he, cigarette in mouth, handled them fearlessly, without mask or gloves.

When my father wasn't working in the orchards, he loved to do things around the house. I remember my mother proudly telling the story of the special lamp he created that used batteries and lit the house much better than a kerosene lamp. "It was before Passover in 1935, just before you entered our lives," she would tell me, smiling. "Your grandmother was so busy with the spring cleaning, painting the walls of the house inside and outside. Your father was always getting in her way, constantly trying to connect the batteries, which he finally did. The lamp became an excellent source of light for us." I loved to hear stories of how wonderful my father was. In the evenings I would sit by his lit lamp, shutting my eyes tightly to see if the smallest streak of light could get inside my closed eyelids.

With his slender build, big blue eyes and dark blond hair, my father was a very handsome man. He and my mother, Sara, first met in Turka when they were both thirteen years old and fell instantly in love. The courtship, which lasted eight years, culminated in their marriage on November 5, 1928, when they were twenty-one years old. After their wedding, my mother moved to the Milbauer farm to live with her new husband and his family.

My mother was not born in Turka. She came from Stanisławów, a neighbouring city. Her early childhood had been tragic and traumatic. Her father, Izydor Weisman, died of diabetes at the age of twenty-six, leaving behind his young wife, Judith Zweig, and two small daughters, Sara, aged six, and Miriam, aged three. Judith came from a very wealthy and prominent family. Her older brother, Leo Zweig, took on the care of his older niece, my mother, Sara. He arranged for her to go to the Baron Hirsch School, a Jewish boarding school in Ahlen, Germany. My mother was an excellent student. She became fluent in German and admired German literature, culture and lifestyle. Due to her musical ability, she soon joined the choir and sang second voice, alto. She spent all her time at the boarding school. She did not even want to go home for summer vacations.

In the meantime, Judith was raising Miriam all alone and although she was financially secure and did not need to work, it was very difficult for her emotionally. She struggled with her loneliness and her friends began to encourage her to accept matchmaking proposals. At first she refused to meet men, but eventually she felt that she needed a companion. At last she met her future husband, Aaron Blaufeld. He was an older widower from the village of Turka who was raising seven children of his own, six sons and one daughter. Her family strongly disapproved of the match. They were concerned about Aaron's advanced age and the responsibilities Judith would be taking on in raising his children. They also did not like the fact that she would have to move to Turka. However, Judith was determined and agreed to marry Aaron and to move, for the first time in her life, to a farm. Once Judith was married, her brother Leo no longer felt the responsibility to support Sara in Germany. When my mother was thirteen, before she had the opportunity to graduate from high school, she was forced to leave her beloved school in Germany and return to Poland.

Chapter 2

After my parents were married, an additional room was built for them onto the living room of the Milbauer farm. There, after the turmoil of her young life, Sara was happy. She had a loving husband who couldn't do enough to please her and who surprised her by making a pond for her, with a narrow path that led to the barn. He stocked the pond with carp, her favourite fish. I remember well the wooden floor of their room, the door that led out onto a large porch overlooking the back garden, and their antique white bedroom set. A colourful kilim that Velvel had made for them hung over their bed and a red wood antique hope chest stood at the foot of the bed.

Sara's first four pregnancies all ended tragically, with the death of each baby shortly after birth. It was not until April 24, 1935, when I was born, that they had a child that survived. I was named Rachel and given the middle name Chai which means "life" in Hebrew. For my Hebrew name, used on Jewish ceremonial occasions, my parents chose Chai Rachel. My grandparents often used my Hebrew name as an endearment.

I adored living on the farm and was in heaven running in the vast green meadows and picking flowers. My favourite flowers were little pink and purple ones, and especially the royal blue cornflowers. Sometimes my mother brought a blanket and we would have a picnic and make wreaths for my hair from the flowers we picked.

I had a young colt who was trained to take me from the house to the fields. My bubbie would feed him sugar cubes, put me on his back and direct him into the fields. I held onto the colt and when I arrived at the fields, my father or Vasil, our farmhand, took me off. Vasil Olehrecky and his wife, Maria, were Ukrainians who worked on our farm. They were a young couple who had no land of their own and were very loyal, honest and likeable people. My family treated them very well and, in return, they worked hard, tending to the animals, maintaining the grounds around the house and chopping firewood for the stove. They were always welcome to take home produce grown on our farm.

Bobby, our dog, was my constant companion. He and I went everywhere together. When I was tired I sat on him like on a pony and he happily carried me around. I used to say that when I grew up and went to school, Bobby would carry my school bag for me. My grandmother would smile and say, "Little Rachel, you still have a long way to go and a lot of bread to eat before you can go to school." I didn't worry. As long as Bobby was beside me and let me hug him to my heart's content, all would be well. My life was blessed.

~

A few years before the outbreak of the war, my mother's sister Miriam, whom we called Aunt Mina, married her stepbrother, Moses Blaufeld. Their farm was on the other side of our village, where there was a large concentration of Jewish families. Some of Moses' siblings had died young and others had married and moved away. As a result, Mina, Moses and their daughter, Luci, who was a year younger than I, had the farm to themselves. At the beginning of 1938, Mina and Sara's mother, Judith, was widowed for the second time. She lived with Mina and her family on their farm. We called her Bubbie Yetta.

My cousin, Luci, was shorter than I. She was chubby and had black curly hair, which she wore pulled back into two short braids. Uncle Moses was often away on business and my mother and I would visit, usually staying overnight. Luci and I slept with Bubbie Yetta while my mother slept with her sister Mina in the bedroom.

There was always plenty to occupy Luci and me during the day. Usually we were busy in the clover field at the back of the house where we spent whole days searching for and picking fourleaf clovers. My favourite thing at their house though, was Bubbie Yetta's flower garden, where I was fascinated by all the flowers, particularly the bleeding hearts.

Strange things always seemed to happen when we were at Luci's house and my visits there became very stressful. Once, Luci and I woke up in the morning shocked to find ourselves and our bed in the middle of the room. Bubbie Yetta ran outside to talk to the neighbours and we discovered there had been an earthquake in the middle of the night. Another time when we stayed over, burglars came by and stole the laundry hanging outside to dry. Bubbie Yetta told us this was the third time that such a thing had happened. "We must have enemies," she said. "What do thieves look like?" I asked. "They have huge eyes and long hands," she informed me, opening her eyes wide and stretching her arms toward me. In my four-year-old mind, I imagined a strange monster-like creature stealing clothes and eating people. It worried and frightened me.

⁓

In the summer of 1939, the adults around me began to seem busy and preoccupied. There was talk of Hitler and the coming war, but my mother and I continued to visit Luci's house as usual. When we arrived, Luci was very happy to see me and we played together, singing and dancing all day long. One morning on one of our visits, we were all awakened by a loud knocking at the door and the sound of shattering glass. We jumped out of bed and dressed quickly, trying to be very quiet. While Bubbie Yetta secured the front and back door locks, Aunt Mina made sure the shutters on the windows were tightly closed. My mother and my aunt moved the big bed away from the window into the middle of the room and all of us, three women and two small children, crawled under the bed. We stayed there for a long time, but the noise of the shattering glass from rocks thrown through the windows did not stop. From outside the door we could hear loud screaming, "Come out, you dirty Jews, come out right now!"

Finally, Mina whispered, "Let's run to the fields through the back-yard since all the noise seems to be coming from the front." Bubbie Yetta said we should all run and that she would stay at home as a decoy. She thought that if the terrorizers broke down the door and found an old woman, they would not go running off to look for others. She would not be deterred, repeating that she was not afraid and would not go with us. There was no time to argue. My mother took me in her arms, Mina took Luci and we ran out the back door.

In our hurry to escape we did not think of putting on our shoes. After we passed the clover field, where the grass reached my knees, my mother put me down so she could run faster and dragged me along beside her, holding my hand. We ran through cornfields, wheat fields and fields of stubble, where we cut our feet so badly they bled. Our feet were extremely painful and Luci and I cried desperately. It was hot and the sun beat down on us. We were thirsty and hungry, and our legs were swollen and covered with blisters and blood. My aunt continued to carry Luci in her arms, while my mother dragged me alongside her. She explained to me later that I was bigger than Luci and that she was very tired, but for the first time in my life I felt separated from my mother. Unprotected. A burden.

We ran for several hours, finally settling down in the fields to hide. We stayed there until evening, when it seemed safe to return. The pain in our feet and bodies was unbearable. Everything seemed quiet when we came to the house and carefully went inside. When my bubbie saw us she jumped up in joy. "Where have you been for so long? I was so worried about you all."

Tearfully, while treating our wounded feet and feeding us warm soup, she explained that shortly after we left the house, the noise subsided and, disappointed at having missed an opportunity to do some serious damage, the hoodlums left. Before we fell asleep in her bed that night, we hugged and kissed our bubbie. Safe again.

~

Our house faced the main road that ran from our village to the city of Kołomyja and stood at the foot of a mountain. In my eyes, at age three and four, our mountain looked huge and very steep, but in reality it was neither. I climbed the mountain often to visit my friends, the three "Mecios." Three Ukrainian families lived on the mountain and each family had a small son. All three boys were named Matthew, or Mecio for short. I loved to play with them. We spoke Ukrainian, even though I spoke only Yiddish at home.

My favourite Mecio was a year older than I. We spent most of our time together. His family lived in the house to the right. The Mecio who was younger than I lived in the middle house and the third Mecio lived on the left. The third Mecio was the eldest and rarely played with us. When the four of us played together it was never for very long, as something would always go wrong. Looking back now, I suppose I was lucky that they consented to play with a girl at all.

Some days, my favourite Mecio came down to visit me and we ran in the fields all day. But most mornings, I climbed our mountain to visit him. The main obstacle to my morning excursions were the turkeys my grandmother raised in the yard. The moment they saw me emerge from the house they ran straight toward me, their beaks aimed at my eyes. I always covered my eyes and screamed, "Bubbie! Bubbie! Come quick!" She came running and chased them away. "They run to you because of your red coat," she would say. "Don't worry, I will protect you." She held me close and hugged and kissed me as I looked up into her eyes. "Go," she would say. "Take your breakfast out and bring it up to Mecio's. You can both share it." And off I went with my little wooden bowl filled with some sunflower seed oil and a chunk of rye bread. Despite the dirt that always seemed to cling to him and his constant runny nose, I loved my favourite Mecio and looked forward to our feasts together.

Winter was as much fun as summer. Zeyde Eli made me a little toboggan and a small pair of skis. I would climb our mountain with my skis and hand one to Mecio. We sat on our skis and zoomed down the mountain. Sometimes I tumbled off at the bottom and my bubbie, who watched me from the window, would run out in a flash to pick me up. It was embarrassing to have her bound out of the house to rescue me while I was playing with my friend. I hated it. She would carry me into the house and sit me down at the table. Being a superstitious woman, always afraid something bad would happen to me, she set about preparing her ritual: melting a little wax in a small pot and pouring it onto a plate to solidify. She said she could read my future in the shapes. It always frightened me to see her doing this because I couldn't understand it. "Bubbie," I would ask, "what do you see in the wax? I don't see anything." Whispering, she would reply, "I see a little dog and a little house and I see you very happy." How was it possible that she could see such things? It had to be a miracle. "Why do you do that?" I asked her. "I do this because I am afraid of the evil eye," she continued. "I'm afraid something bad will happen to you." This terrified me and I cried, "Stop it, Bubbie, I am afraid of this. How can you see that if it is invisible?" At that point, seeing my terror, she would give up her wax reading. I was more afraid of the little piece of wax than I was of falling down the mountain. My only way out was to try my best not to fall.

~

I was a very poor eater. There were only two meals I would agree to eat. Bubbie would give me a little bowl with homemade sunflower seed oil, into which I dipped her rye bread. Sometimes I ate a slice of bread spread with butter and sprinkled with sugar. Bubbie tried everything to get me to eat, even involving me in the preparation of the meals. She often cooked beans of different kinds and asked me to help sort them from the dirt before cooking. Unfortunately, I was more interested in helping than in eating. She also invited my friends, who were good eaters, for meals, thinking that I would watch them and, by example, eat as well. It never worked.

My mother became angry when I refused to drink milk from the goat we had on the farm. Bubbie often gave me chocolate with the goat's milk and my mother refused to let me eat the chocolate if I didn't drink the glass of milk with it. When she threatened to take the chocolate away, I indignantly returned the melting pieces to her, my hands covered in melted chocolate, and angrily told her I didn't want anything at all. That made her very upset and she scolded me for dirtying my embroidered blouse. Looking sternly at me she would say, "You are as stubborn as a mule." I would glare back at her, not liking the remark, and wonder who was more stubborn. Neither I nor anyone else realized then that soon we would all be starving.

Part Two:
War, Survival, Silence

Chapter 3

In the fall of 1939, six months before my fifth birthday, the Soviet army occupied our area of Poland. The war with Germany had already advanced into the western and central parts of Poland. Soon after, the Soviets began mobilizing young men into the army, and my father was among those drafted.[3]

Everything at home changed after my father left. I was not allowed to be happy or to smile. We often heard planes overhead and I would ask, "Is my daddy in that plane?" "Oh, yes," my bubbie would answer, and that made me so proud. When I played with my friends or Luci, and a plane flew overhead, I would point to the sky and scream, "My daddy is there. Quick, look up!" I talked to him in my mind and said, "Daddy, I miss you, come home." It was a very difficult time for me. As weeks turned to months, and months to more than a year, I often thought I would never see my father again. Soon, I no longer had to be reminded to be sad and I told Luci that she could not laugh until my father came home.

---

3 On August 24, 1939, the USSR and Germany signed the Treaty of Non-aggression. This treaty, also known as the Molotov-Ribbentrop Pact, included a secret protocol in which Poland was divided between the USSR and Germany. On September 1, 1939, Germany invaded Poland from the west. In keeping with the terms of the pact, the Soviet Union invaded from the east on September 17, 1939. The author's village of Turka was located in the part of Poland occupied by the Soviet Union.

Things began to deteriorate very quickly when Germany attacked the USSR.[4] My zeyde and my uncles were constantly involved in heated discussions. They had a very important decision to make. The Soviets had promised to supply transportation to all those who wanted to move further east into the USSR. My uncle Velvel tried to convince my zeyde that we should go. "The Germans are moving quickly toward the east. Now is the time and this is the opportunity for us to move," he begged. But my zeyde wouldn't listen. "What? Are you crazy? You want me to leave everything we possess and go away – to where?" He waved his hand at them, signalling he was through with talk. "This war," he concluded, "won't last more than a few weeks at most." His sons could not convince him, though they tried many times.

~

We continued to live in our house for some time after the German attack on the USSR. We had no word from my father. My zeyde continued to teach me the Hebrew alphabet and never stopped hoping for better times, but there was no more talk of a speedy end to the war. Zeyde kept praying. He said, "The world will not allow the destruction of innocent people and children. There is a God, and He will take care of us. He will not let us down and we have to trust in Him."

Our visits to Luci became rare and the stress at home grew by the day. The frontline of the war between Germany and the USSR was getting closer to us. Some of my family's non-Jewish neighbours and friends became distant and not as friendly. Antisemitism was felt everywhere. No one wanted to buy our farm goods and only our hired farm labourers, Vasil and Maria Olehrecky, remained with us. Others abandoned us for seemingly no reason at all. Our joyful home

---

4 On June 22, 1941, Germany broke the Treaty of Non-aggression with the USSR by invading Soviet territory. The author's village was close to the initial fighting.

had turned into a house filled with sadness and fear. We kept our windows shut and our doors barred at all times.

When the Hungarian army, allied with Germany, invaded Kołomyja in July 1941, my mother, who was regarded as a very intelligent and knowledgeable person in our village, was working as the editor-in-chief of the newspaper in our area.[5] There were a few other Jews and some Ukrainians working there with her. Working at the paper helped her cope with my father's absence. The newspaper gave her access to first-hand news of the progression of the war and afforded her a sense of control over a life she felt crumbling beneath her. She continued to work at the paper even after all her other Jewish co-workers had fled on Soviet trucks.

In August 1941, soon after the Germans had occupied Kołomyja, my mother did not come home from work one day. When Shiko went to find out what had happened to her, he was told that she was in custody and that, if she did not give up the names of the other Jewish employees who had worked at the newspaper and fled, they were going to kill her and her family. Shiko begged the Germans to let her go. He told them that she had a small child. They were not moved and he was lucky to escape the headquarters with his own life. What they did not tell him, what we later learned from my mother, was that the Gestapo – the German political police – had by then already tortured her into unconsciousness. When she lost consciousness, they poured water on her to revive her and continued beating and interrogating her, hoping that she would betray her colleagues. Bleeding, and having lost several teeth, my mother still refused to speak. Finally, they threw her into a dark, mouse-infested cellar.

We were frantic and frightened for my mother, who had lately become so fragile, thin and weak. We all hoped that her excellent

---

5   On July 3, 1941, the last Soviet troops pulled out of Kołomyja and the surrounding areas. The next day, Hungarian troops, allied with Nazi Germany, occupied the area and remained there for six weeks until the German Wehrmacht took over.

German would help her convince the Gestapo to let her go. But after three days had passed and she had still not returned home, Uncle Shiko prepared the horse and carriage and took me to see my mother. When we arrived, they brought her up from the cellar. When I saw her, I began to scream uncontrollably. I could not recognize my own mother's face.

There were two Ukrainian men present at the prison whom my mother knew from before the war. They were Nazi collaborators. In a moment of what I suppose was remorse, one of them whispered something to the Gestapo. A few minutes later, one of the Germans shouted to my uncle, "Take her and get out of here – for now!" I don't know what the Ukrainian said, or why it affected the police, but they let my mother go. My mother always said that it was I who saved her life.

From that point on, the Jews were continually persecuted. In November 1941, Jews from villages and farms surrounding Kołomyja were forced to relocate into the city, where soon a ghetto was established.[6]

---

6 The Kołomyja ghetto was officially established and fully closed off from the rest of the city in late March 1942. As was the pattern with all the ghettos established by the Nazis in Poland, the first stage toward the creation of the ghetto was the forcible resettlement of the population from nearby rural areas. Rachel and her family were forced to move to Kołomyja in November 1941.

Chapter 4

On the morning we were forced to leave our home, our farm and our animals, we awoke to silence. We had locked the doors and windows securely the night before and Bobby, our dog, had been sleeping outside. But Bobby was not barking that morning – I never heard or saw him again. At the crack of dawn, the Germans had surrounded our house and were waiting for us to get up. When Bubbie Frida stepped outside, her greatest fear was realized.

"Get out, you filthy Jews."

German police stood in our yard, pointing guns at us and shouting in German. My bubbie, who knew a little German, asked if I could go up the mountain and say goodbye to my friend. Strangely, they agreed. My bubbie whispered to me, "Stay up there. Don't come back." So I ran up the mountain to say goodbye. When I was ready to leave Mecio, his mother told me she would come down with me and ask permission to keep me with her family. The answer she got from the Germans was short and to the point. "No. Get out of here." Hurriedly, my bubbie put a few of her dresses into a small suitcase and we were chased out of our home, forced to leave everything else behind.

As they pushed us into the road, my zeyde, who had remembered to take his prayer book, realized he had forgotten his eyeglasses on the windowsill. He started back to the house to get them. One of the Germans kicked him and he fell to the ground. As he lay on the dirt road, another German pulled as hard as he could at his beard. My zeyde, moaning in pain, began to lose consciousness. With what appeared to me to be enjoyment, the German police continued to pull at each strand of my zeyde's beard. When they had pulled out almost all of his long beautiful beard, they cut with a knife what they could not pull out with their hands. I closed my eyes and hid myself between my mother and my bubbie.

Hungry, thirsty and stunned, we were ordered to walk in the direction of Kołomyja. As we stumbled toward the town, we were joined by other Jewish families. If anyone stepped out of line or tried to escape, they were immediately shot. My uncles took turns carrying me. At the time, it seemed a miracle that we all made it to Kołomyja alive. There, we were reunited with friends from the surrounding areas and with Aunt Mina and Luci. I was six years old.

The Kołomyja ghetto was located in the central part of the city, near the farmers' market where peasants from the surrounding villages used to gather to sell their goods. This particular area and some of the nearby houses were ringed by a gate that separated it from the rest of the city. The non-Jewish families who lived there had been evacuated and given the vacated houses of Jews outside the ghetto walls. The Jewish families who lived inside the gated ghetto remained in their homes, but had to share them with Jews who were brought in from elsewhere.

Armed with rifles, the soldiers stood at the gateway, policing the Jews in the ghetto. We were forced to wear armbands with embroidered Stars of David on them. Our shoes were taken away and a strict curfew was imposed. Those who disobeyed were shot on the spot. For the first time in my life I knew what fear really was.

My family was lucky to have been placed together. Bubbie Yetta, Aunt Mina, Uncle Moses, Luci, my mother and I shared one little room, along with our close family friends from Turka, Baruch Ertenstreich, his wife and his mother. The room the nine of us shared was dark, except for one small window. We had only one small table, two chairs, an iron stove and wooden planks for beds. The other members of my family – Zeyde Eli, Bubbie Frida and Uncles Velvel and Shiko – were housed in the little room next to ours. They shared the room with Mendel Milbauer (Zeyde's brother), Mendel's wife and two daughters, and a family friend from Turka, Dr. Nieder.

My family, who had always been as familiar to me as I was to myself, became unrecognizable. The German police had torn away Zeyde Eli's beard and moustache. Bubbie Frida's loving face had become sad and helpless. Her beautiful blue eyes were now always filled with tears and fear. As we all sat, day in and day out, in this dark, small room on plank beds, my safe and comfortable world began to disintegrate around me. Often I would try to escape and remember our life on the farm: my handsome zeyde at home in Turka, reading the Torah, no concern for the outside world; me, running around the farm without a care and full of joy; my bubbie – so busy, so full of life.

My thoughts flew back to our last day on the farm when the German police had surrounded our house and how my bubbie's first thought had been to save me. In German, she had begged them to let me go up the mountain to say my goodbyes. As I began to run she had shouted to me in Ukrainian, so that the Germans would not understand, to stay up there and not come back.

Sitting on my mother's lap on the plank bed, I tried to sneak glances at her face. She looked so lonely and trapped, helpless and silent. Suddenly and in such a short time, she had aged, her cheeks sunken, her eyes filled with panic. When I asked her about my father, whether he was alive and if he would be able to find us, she tried to comfort me. "We have to pray for him," she would say, "so that he will come and find us here." As I held onto her and clutched at her arms, I remembered how beautiful she had always looked to me.

Uncle Shiko spent most of his time pacing the floor, rubbing his hands together nervously, and speaking in half sentences to Dr. Nieder. He looked to me like a bird trapped in a cage. Uncle Velvel, on the other hand, was quiet. Just like me. When his eyes met mine he would tell me not to be frightened or worried. He assured me that I would survive it all. "A trace of us has to remain," he would whisper, "and you will be that one. You will make it." It was Velvel's words that made me feel safer. I trusted him.

Sometimes, late at night when I could not sleep, I dreamt of the special times in Kołomyja. During celebrations and weddings, the townspeople, who had their own folk music, songs, dances and costumes, wore their beautiful traditional dress. They even had a song and dance called the Kołomyjka, which everyone knew and that was passed down from generation to generation. Girls, their heads adorned with fresh-flower wreaths and brightly coloured ribbons, were spectacular in their hand-embroidered blouses, vests, richly gathered skirts and shiny bead necklaces. The men, dressed like the local Hutzul mountain men, wore embroidered white shirts over their pants, bright, hand-woven cloth belts around their waists, colourfully embroidered vests and black cloth hats with showy feathers on one side. The special character of the city Kołomyja was so dear to me.

I dreamt of Jewish holidays like Sukkoth, with all of us gathered in the *sukkah* on my parents' porch for meals. I loved the way the walls were decorated with leaves and branches and how I could watch the countless stars in the sky from the roofless room. Even though I could hardly count to ten back then, I would count the stars over and over again. My bubbie would dress me in a navy blue pleated skirt and white embroidered blouse, and I was always the first one ready and seated when it was time for dinner. I can still hear her voice. "Rachel, you are my life and my world. You are so good and so sweet and I love you."

Chapter 5

Life in the ghetto was very difficult. Our living space was quickly permeated with horrible smells from trash and human waste. The few clothes that we had were dirty and torn. We could not bathe. Our shoeless feet were soiled and swollen and covered with blisters.

Men and women who were young and strong were sent out of the ghetto to do hard labour, like building and repairing roadways. Some had to carry large, heavy rocks, while others had to cut the large rocks into smaller pieces by hand. The work was very hard and was done under the strict, watchful eyes of the guards. There was constant change inside the ghetto, with Jews arriving from surrounding cities, towns and villages as others were being sent away by train. At the time we thought they were being sent to work. They never came back. We later found out they were sent to concentration camps.

Each morning, the soldiers rounded up the Jews in the ghetto. Then, they randomly selected who would be tortured and murdered that day. The German police rotated their selections daily, choosing either children of a certain age group, adults, the elderly or the ill and disabled. These murders were carried out in front of us as we stood horrified, imagining ourselves in the place of those poor souls who had been selected. One never knew who would be next. I was in constant fear for my family and for my own life.

During one particular roundup, I was indoors with Bubbie Yetta when we heard petrifying screams. We ran outside to witness the selection of that day. Six boys, bar-mitzvah age (thirteen years old), had been forced down on the ground in the shape of a Star of David. The SS cut off their ears and noses, broke their fingers, and poked out their eyes. Finally, their screams were silenced by bullets. Breathless and trembling, I held onto Bubbie Yetta's skirt. "Please stop it," I prayed. "Somebody help us." For weeks afterward, I waited in fear. Waited for my turn.

~

Luci and I spent most of our time in the ghetto collecting vegetable peels from the garbage. Our hunger was so great that potato and onion peels or any other rotten vegetables became treasures. We rolled up our dresses and put the scraps of the day in our skirts, and Bubbie Yetta made soup out of our finds.

I forced myself to think about home on the farm. The back of our property in Turka was on a slight hill, at the bottom of which there was a little stream that divided the meadow and stretched from our side of the property to the other. Over the stream, connecting the two sides of the meadow, there was a small wooden footbridge. A family of Gypsies who had set up camp in tents lived on the other side of the stream. The older Gypsy man had set up a blacksmith shop in an old, neglected barn nearby and when my zeyde needed to have the horses' shoes replaced, he took them to the Gypsy's blacksmith shop. Zeyde always invited me along and I was glad to stop whatever I was doing to run and join him. I loved going to the Gypsy camp. I would watch the men hold the iron in the hot flames until it became red. Then they knocked the iron with a big hammer to shape it into a horseshoe until finally fitting the repaired shoe onto our horse. In exchange for the blacksmith work, Zeyde gave the Gypsy man eggs, chickens and other foods.

~

It often felt as though chance and fate were playing a larger part in our survival than anything else. Some say that it is the will to live that allows those in danger to survive, but I am not sure. While some people were shot for seemingly no reason at all, others managed to escape such a fate. Why?

One bitterly cold morning, I stood beside my mother during a roundup. Shivering with cold and fear, we stood close together as two Gestapo officers moved in our direction. They stopped at a fair distance, called out my mother's name and ordered her to step out of line and walk forward. I may have been little, but I knew what that meant. As she began to move, I quickly reached for her ice-cold hand and walked with her. I was six years old and the thought of my mother dying alone was unimaginable. Frantically, my mother tried to push me back, but I held on tight. We walked slowly and finally came to a stop. I closed my eyes. "How would it feel to die?" I wondered. "Would it be very painful? Where would the bullet hit us?"

As we approached, one of the Gestapo officers asked my mother if she could speak German. When she answered in German that she spoke fluently, they ordered her to follow them. She asked to be allowed to bring her daughter along and we followed the Germans to the ghetto gate and beyond. We came to a stop in front of Jacob's house. Jacob was my mother's cousin who had been a tailor of men's clothing before the war. The Nazis had allowed him to stay in his home in Kołomyja, outside the ghetto, so that he could sew uniforms for the Gestapo officers. Jacob, however, spoke only Polish and Yiddish. He had asked them to bring his cousin Sara Milbauer, who could easily translate for him. And so my mother and I found ourselves living with Jacob. We were saved. For now.

Jacob had a large room with sewing machines and mannequins. He worked long, hard hours to stay in the Nazis' favour. My mother would sit beside Jacob, helping him stitch by hand, and translate for the Gestapo who came in frequently to try on their uniforms. They were pleased with my mother's services. At night, my mother and I slept in a bed in the workshop and Jacob slept in the kitchen.

As far as the Germans were concerned, it was only the three of us living in the house, but Jacob had made a hiding place in the kitchen beneath the wooden floor under his bed. In the daytime, while he worked, his wife and two young sons hid under the floor. Late at night, he brought them out so that they could fill their lungs with air, have something to eat and sleep on the floor in the kitchen. We were thankful. To have a place to sleep. Air to breathe. I was thankful to be safe and alive with my mother.

Chapter 6

Before my mother and I went to live with Jacob, my bubbie Frida's sister had a heart attack. When she passed away, much to our surprise, the authorities permitted us to hold a funeral for her in the Jewish cemetery. Under the paralyzing eyes of the SS, Bubbie Frida and some other family members walked slowly toward the spot where they believed they would bury my great-aunt.

Zeyde Eli was a *cohen* and, according to Jewish law, he was not allowed to enter the cemetery. He stood near the fence and observed the funeral from afar. He was quite a distance from the mourners, so he watched them walk slowly and could only see their lips moving but could not hear the words. Lost in thought, saying the prayer for the dead under his breath, Zeyde noticed the mourners begin to dig graves. Then, he watched as the SS commanded them to bury each other – alive – in the graves they had dug. Those who refused were shot to death on the spot where they stood.

"The graves were moving," Zeyde Eli cried, as he ran back to the ghetto where Bubbie Yetta, my mother and I were waiting for the mourners to return. "I watched my wife, my Frida, buried alive!" he wailed. Within a month of Frida's death, Zeyde Eli passed away.

Chapter 7

One night, as my mother and I slept, Jacob pulled his family out of the hiding place so they could sleep on the floor. Suddenly, there was a desperate knock at the door. Immediately, Jacob pushed his wife and sons back into their hiding place and pulled his bed over it. My mother ran to the window and jumped from the second floor to the ground. I was stunned and petrified. I heard loud male voices shouting in broken German, "Father! Mother! Write!" It did not make any sense to me or to Jacob. With great fear he went to the door and let the men in. There were three tall men dressed in black uniforms pointing guns at us. They spread out through the workshop like wild animals. One of them came to my bed and began to stab the bed with a dagger. Another pointed his gun at Jacob and pushed him into the kitchen. They kept repeating the sentence, "Father! Mother! Write!" They seemed to be speaking in broken German, but their native tongue was a mystery.[7]

I was sure they would kill us. Finally, Jacob opened a drawer in the kitchen cupboard and gave them some jewellery, money and his

---

7 The men, apparently Hungarian police, mispronounced the German verb for "get down to action" or "get going" – *schreiten* – with the verb for "to write" – *schreiben*.

wristwatch. They grabbed it all and rushed out. Jacob told me he thought they were Hungarian police who had come to rob us, that we had been very lucky and that, thankfully, he had found something he could give them. Suddenly, he stopped talking and looked around. "Where is your mother?" he asked. "She's gone. She jumped through the window," I sobbed. I was sure she was dead. Jacob took me in his arms and held me tight, as he whispered into my hair, "Don't worry. Mommy will come back."

Jacob held me all night. But neither of us could sleep. I could see the desperation on his ghost-like face and he could feel my trembling. At dawn, there was another knock at the door. Jacob quickly let my mother in and locked the door behind her. He stared at her in disbelief. "Sara, where have you been all night?" She looked pale and weak and she was shivering with cold. "I went to warn the other Jewish families and I hid in the dark. I was afraid to come back." "But you could have been killed jumping from so high," Jacob replied. "And how could you have left your child alone?" I could see the astonishment on his face.

I only cared that she had come back. I hugged her and kissed her face. Sobbing, I begged her, "Don't ever leave me again, Mommy." In my heart, a strange pang stabbed at me. It didn't make sense. When my mother was called out by the Gestapo in the ghetto and I thought she was going to be killed, I, at the age of six, had stepped out of line just to be with her. In the face of grave danger, she had left me alone, possibly to die.

Chapter 8

The Nazis continued to come often to the workshop, demanding that Jacob speed up his work. One of Jacob's customers was a young German pilot stationed in Kołomyja. He took a liking to my mother and would stay for hours, discussing German literature with her, particularly the poems of Goethe, which my mother could recite by heart. My mother was polite to him. She hoped that he would like her, not because she had any feelings for him, but because she was desperately hoping he would help us during those terrible times. She felt that he was the only shred of hope for our survival at that point. He would call me to sit on his lap when there were no other Germans around, but I always struggled and ran away. Sometimes he brought me chocolate or some little toy. When he was ready to leave, my mother would walk with him to the corridor to let him out. Occasionally, I would sneak to the hallway, watching as he kissed my mother goodbye.

Early one morning, the German pilot came by Jacob's shop. He was very upset. When my mother walked with him to the hallway, he told her nervously that he was being transferred to Paris, France in four days. He wanted her to come with him. He said he could arrange for my mother and me to join him there. "No," my mother answered. "My family is here." The pilot told my mother that the ghetto was going to be liquidated and that no Jew would be left alive. He wanted to save her. "Please," he begged, "think about it. I will come one more time before I leave and I will expect a positive answer." He hugged and kissed my mother and picked me up in his arms and hugged me too. Before he left, he turned around and whispered to my mother, "Your husband will not return. He is most likely dead by now. Don't wait for him. Save yourself." Then he turned and walked out.

When my mother told Jacob what the pilot had said, Jacob was petrified at the horrible news. He could not believe the terrible fate that was awaiting us. It was obvious that the war was far from over. It was also clear that my mother had made her decision. Two days later, the pilot came again and brought me some chocolate. He looked into my mother's eyes and asked, "Well, Sara, will you come with me?" "Thank you very much for your kindness," my mother told him. "If I survive I will always remember you." "But Sara," he continued, "you will not survive. Trust me." "Whatever happens to the rest of the Jews will happen to me as well," she said. "I am staying with my family and with my people." The pilot hugged us both and left. We sat together in the room, sobbing quietly.

A short time later, the Gestapo ordered us to return to the ghetto. Jacob, his family, my mother and I found ourselves reunited with Bubbie Yetta, Aunt Mina, Uncle Moses, Velvel and Shiko, who were, gratefully, still alive. Our friend Baruch was still with us, but his wife and mother had been taken away. I was happiest of all to see Luci, and I promised myself that we would never be separated again.

Chapter 9

One evening in the spring of 1942, my mother returned to our little room after building roads all day. She was exhausted, pale and on the verge of collapse. As we lay in our beds in the desperate darkness of those nights, I knew that my mother and I were both praying for the same thing: my father's safe return. We had all been asleep for quite some time when there was a muffled knock at the door. When Bubbie Yetta opened the door a man staggered in. Exhausted, he sat down on the floor and asked for water. His clothes were torn and his face was overgrown with hair. He was unrecognizable. Could it be?

I remembered that my father had a little bump the size of a pea under the skin of his cheek. I reached for his face with my small hands and felt with my fingers, like a blind child searching for recognition. My father's face. "It's him," I whispered, "It's Daddy!"

The three of us clung to each other for what seemed forever, crying in disbelief. I truly believed that the nightmares were about to end. Everything that had felt so separate and disjointed became fused. The fear and loneliness that I felt in the ghetto, the uncertainty of my mother's loyalty – all of it dissipated. My father had returned.

We learned that my father had been with the Soviet army fighting the Germans and proceeding west toward the German-occupied areas of Poland. When his battalion had reached the city of Chelm, they were captured by the Germans and taken as prisoners of war. My father realized at once that he could not disclose that he was a Jew, so he gave them a Ukrainian name. With his small, straight nose, big blue eyes, round face and blond hair, he did not fit the Jewish stereotype and the Germans were not suspicious. From the beginning, the Germans had problems communicating with the Russians. As my father could speak German, they used him as a translator. He spent many months in captivity, with little hope of freedom. The only chance any of them had was to escape.

There was a storm the night my father and a fellow prisoner escaped. Lightning and thunder surrounded them as they sneaked out of the barracks. They ran through ditches, fields and footpaths at night, and hid in roadside ditches during the day. As they ran in the direction of Kołomyja, they knew they might not succeed in reaching their destination. In desperation, they ate the raw flesh of dead horses lying in the ditches and fields. It took them many months to reach Kołomyja, and when they arrived they parted company. My father knew that the Jews were in the ghetto. Even though he could have saved himself by continuing on, he stepped into the hell of the ghetto to find us. Now we were reunited. The next morning when the work crews left for hard labour on the roads, my father was with them.

Chapter 10

In the summer of 1942, circumstances began to change for us. The Germans decided to send all the young men and women to the village of Turka to work in the fields. Surprisingly, Bubbie Yetta was included along with my parents. The day before my family was to go to work in the fields, my father and Uncle Moses discussed how to sneak Luci and me out of the ghetto. They feared that if they left us behind they would not find us when they returned. Our parents then prepared us for the dangerous journey. Luci and I were to be put into knapsacks containing farm and garden tools and my father and Moses would carry us on their backs out of the ghetto.

Early the next morning, my father packed me into the bag, arranged the tools around me and lifted me onto his shoulder. I tried to shrink myself into a little ball inside the bag. I was afraid and stifled with not enough air to breathe. At the gate, the guard poked at my father's knapsack with his dagger. It hurt, but I did not make a sound and held my breath.

So far, the escape had been successful. When we arrived at the village of Turka, each family got a barracks and a plank bed. My father immediately emptied me out of the bag and sent me under the bed. Moses did the same with Luci. Our parents told us to stay under the beds as long as they were at work. When they returned, we could come out and sleep with them on the plank bed. Early each morning, they sent us into hiding. "Remember," they would tell us, "the German guards can see you and if they catch you, they will kill you."

The days were long and boring. The beds were so low we could not even sit up under them. And we could not speak out loud, only whisper. The barracks had a little window and from beneath the bed we could see the sun shining a little in the room. After several weeks of this hidden life we had both had enough. We were hungry and terribly bored. We decided that it would be fine if we got out from under the bed every day and jumped around a little bit in the room. We did not tell our parents and the plan worked – for a while.

One afternoon, while we were dancing around the room, a German guard spotted us. He came into the barracks like thunder and pointed his gun at us. Shaking and trembling, we both started to cry. All I could think was that our parents would be so angry. I knew that I was older than Luci and should have known better. How could I have not obeyed them? Suddenly, I felt the back of the German soldier's boot as he kicked us both and we flew out the door. We were crying loudly, hoping that someone would hear and help us. The guard looked at me and Luci clinging to each other and, strangely, touched my long blond braids. He had decided not to kill us. He ordered one of the guards to take us to Kołomyja. The guard dumped us onto the street of the ghetto and we just sat there among all the dead bodies, whimpering. I was certain that my parents would never find me. What would they think when they returned not to find us in the barracks? What would happen to us?

The next morning, when my father went to work in the fields, he made contact with a farmer he knew in the adjacent field. Jozef Beck was someone my father had known before the war and he begged him to help. He asked Jozef to go to the ghetto and find us. He asked him to save us if he could and keep us hidden at his farm. Mr. Beck took his horse and carriage and went into the ghetto. He told the guards that he had come to take away some of the corpses. They agreed to let him in. He spotted us, sitting where we had been dumped the day before, in the middle of the street. Luci and I watched as he piled some of the dead bodies on the carriage and then quickly he picked us up and threw us on top, covering us with more dead bodies. When the carriage was full, he drove us out of the ghetto.

Jozef drove to the cemetery and dropped everything onto the ground, including Luci and me. Quickly, he fished us out of the pile and propelled us behind the biggest tombstone he could find. "Tonight," he told us, "my wife, Rozalia, will come to fetch you and take you to our home. You will sit here quietly until it is dark. And do not move. Do you promise?" We promised.

Alone and petrified, crouching behind tombstones and surrounded by corpses, Luci and I waited for Jozef's wife. Every sound of the crackling leaves and the howling wind sounded like footsteps. From time to time, I peeked out from behind our tombstone to see if someone was coming, terrified that I was stepping on Bubbie Frida's dead body under my feet. I tried to occupy my mind with other thoughts and resumed my vigil for Rozalia. It seemed as if we had been sitting there forever, huddled behind the tombstone when, finally, we heard someone walking through the darkness. A woman, bundled up and wearing a huge black shawl on her head, made her way toward us carrying blankets. As she approached, she whispered to us that she was Rozalia. She told us not to be afraid. She took us by the hand and led us out of the cemetery to her waiting horse and carriage.

Chapter 11

The barn on the Becks' farm was piled high with straw and hay. Rozalia settled us on the upper level on a huge pile of straw and spoke sternly to us. "I have six children," she said, "so no one can know that you are here. If the Germans discover that you are hiding here, we will all be killed. You must be quiet and promise to behave. Don't move! Do you understand?" She gave us each a piece of bread and covered us with a blanket.

Weeks passed. The days and nights became indistinguishable. We could hear the Beck children playing in the barn or outside. We longed to join them, but we remained motionless and silent. Luci cried all the time. At seven, a year older than Luci, I felt as though I had to be strong and responsible. I did everything I could to try to calm her. Neglecting and suppressing my own fears in order to stay alive, I invented a game. There was a wooden ledge that held the straw on the upper level of the barn from falling. I told Luci that we were going to spit on the ledge. If our two drops of saliva joined together it would mean that soon our parents would come and get us. If the saliva drops did not join, then we would have to wait longer. It was hard to produce so many drops of saliva and our mouths soon became very dry. The game was not working.

On one particular morning, Luci and I woke to feel sun rays on our faces. The barn, otherwise sullen and dark, felt bright for the first time. Two of the Beck daughters, Zofia and Danuta, were playing in the barn and, unintentionally, we moved and they spotted us. They were older than we were and quickly deduced that we were Jewish children hiding in the barn. They called to us and told us to come down and play with them. Our joy was indescribable. We jumped at the chance to move around and play. We had almost forgotten what it was like to be normal. When they finally left the barn, we scurried back to our hiding place and our silent, motionless existence. The next day, however, we did not see the children. After a few days, one of the girls came running into the barn and called out to us to come down. "Come down here. Hurry! I just saw the Germans coming down the road. They have their guns pointed at your parents. Come down and see for yourselves."

"No!" we screamed in panic and jumped out into the yard. Stunned and relieved, we saw that there was nobody there. She had made a mistake. Suddenly, Mr. Beck was upon us. He grabbed us, enraged, and threw us into the old rose bushes that grew in his front yard. The sharp thorns scratched our emaciated arms and legs, which were now stinging. He dragged us back to the barn. "What are you doing?" he yelled. "You have to be careful and stay very still. Do you know how dangerous this is?" Alone and terrified, Luci and I sat very still, blood dripping down our arms and legs, crying for our parents.

After that, Jozef sought out my father in the fields and told him that to have us on his farm had become too dangerous for his own family. My father would have to come and get us. It was the autumn of 1942 and the work in the fields would soon be over. My father knew that to go back to the ghetto meant certain death. He was sure that within a few months the ghetto would be liquidated and not one Jew would be left alive. He told Jozef he would come get us, and he began to formulate a plan of escape.

~

When my father approached Velvel with his plan, Velvel refused to join him. "I will be of more use here with Uncle Mendel and his family. They are so lost and helpless, I feel like I am the only glue they have to hold them together. Besides," he told my father, "there will be too many of us escaping at once. The Nazis will catch on. Go ahead with your plan," he suggested. "I will try to escape later on."

Instead of going back to the barracks at the end of the day, my father, mother and other members of my family stayed in the tobacco field. Lying motionless until nightfall when they could run more easily without being seen, they waited. That night, my father and Moses made their way to the farm where Luci and I were hiding. Rozalia was waiting for them. She told my father she had a relative in another village who was childless and would agree to take me. It would ensure my survival. My parents were faced with a grave decision. Should they give me up to a gentile family or risk my life by taking me with them?

"She is blond," Rozalia told my father. "She doesn't look Jewish. We'll call her Rose. It is a shame for her to die." My father told her that he would have to talk to his wife before he could give her an answer. My mother, though, did not have to think very long. "Without each other, none of our lives are worth living." I was to stay with my parents. My father enfolded me in his arms. Was it really him? Or was I dreaming? "Don't worry, my little one," my father whispered. "You are safe now. With me and with your mother. We will find a better hiding place where we can all be together." Great relief. I put my head on my father's shoulder and wrapped my arms around his body. I was a child again. I held on for dear life.

⁓

It was at this time, in the late autumn of 1942, that my family and Luci's family separated. My parents and I, Shiko, Baruch Ertenstreich and Dr. Nieder went to Vasil and Maria Olehrecky's farm. They were the couple who had worked on my grandfather's farm. They knew us well and were eager to help us. Vasil settled us under the roof in the attic of their barn and brought food and cigarettes. The straw roof was very old and weak. When the wind blew, even softly, pieces of the roof flew off and small spaces of sky took their place.

As beautiful as it was to have sunlight and to sometimes be able to see a star through the roof at night, we feared that if the roof fell apart we would be discovered. In vain, Vasil tried to fix the roof several times, but he was not successful. Winter was coming, and we were cold and afraid. Without a proper roof, we feared that the peasants from the village would spot us or that we would freeze to death.

In addition, the barn was infested with mice. Our clothes were torn and very dirty, and our bodies were covered with lice. Uncontrollably, I would scratch my head so hard that my scalp bled. Even if the Germans did not discover us, we all knew that we would not survive the winter in this barn. My father would clasp the gun with the ten bullets he had kept at his side since his escape from German captivity and say, "If we fall into the hands of the Germans, I will shoot each one of you and then myself." We lived in constant fear. How many ways are there to say that? After a time, those words become meaningless and finding new ways to describe how it felt to hide in a barn with a failing roof in the middle of the winter, awaiting certain death, is almost impossible.

Dr. Nieder, who was hiding with us, had a Polish girlfriend, Jadwiga. He ventured out at night from our hiding place to meet her in the fields. He never told her where he was hiding, but he received newspapers and reports of the progress of the war from her. We learned that the Germans were now drafting young men in occupied Poland, non-Jews, for work in Germany, young men like Vasil. He knew that he could hide to escape the order as others had done, but that if he did, the Germans would come looking for him and they would find all of us. He decided to report voluntarily to the German authorities.

The night before he left, Vasil came to say goodbye. "I told my wife to take care of you and I will write letters from Germany to see if you are all right," Vasil told my father. "I will refer to you as my brother Peter and I will send you cigarettes. Just try to be hopeful. One day the war will be over and everything will be okay again." My father did not know what to say to this man who was putting himself in harm's way to help us, how to thank him. "I am sorry to have to put you through this. You are young and don't have any children yet. You could hide. Maybe we should find another place." "No! You stay here," Vasil replied curtly. "You do not deserve a life like this. You are decent people and have always been good to my wife and me. If I can save you and you will all be alive when the war is over, this will be my reward." My father and Vasil hugged and cried together.

That night felt very long. Vasil stayed with us in the barn until morning. My father tried to convince him not to go, that we could find another hiding place, but Vasil would not hear of it. He knew that there was no place for us to go. Vasil left, but he kept his word. From Germany, he wrote letters to his wife and his brother "Peter." Maria brought my father the letters and the cigarettes Vasil had sent to him. Vasil risked his marriage, his wife's life and his own life to save ours.

Chapter 12

It was winter, in early 1943. We were freezing and sick with high fevers. Maria Olehrecky, lonely for male company after Vasil left the farm, began having a lot of visitors at night. We could see the men coming and going, which petrified us. Our barn with no roof, where we were afraid even to whisper, was no longer safe.

My father decided that the next snowstorm would be our signal for escape. Looking for another shelter, my father ventured over to Jozef Becks' to ask about my uncle Velvel, who had remained behind in the ghetto. Jozef told my father that Velvel was very sick with typhus. He promised my father that he would watch out for Velvel whenever he could.

Finally the night arrived. We ventured out into a storm, leaving behind the little ruined barn that had become our home. My father knew that Moses, Mina, Bubbie Yetta and Luci were hiding in a barn that belonged to another couple, Vasil and Paraska Hapiuk. Since we had no other place to go, we decided to try our luck and go there. It was risky because joining the others in the Hapiuk barn would mean there would now be a total of ten people hiding there. It was snowing very hard and my father carried me in his arms all the way. As we walked through the cold, snowy night my father kept repeating to himself, "I still have ten bullets."

We could hardly breathe as we stumbled silently toward the farm.

Watching to make sure that everyone was asleep, we crept slowly into the barn. In Yiddish, my father whispered, "It is me, Israel." The barn was very dark and full of straw and hay.

Slowly, a bundle began to move. From behind one bale of straw, the eyes of our family shone in the darkness.

⁓

Vasil and Paraska Hapiuk lived with their son and daughter-in-law, who knew about the four people that Vasil sheltered in the barn. One day, when Vasil brought food, he told Uncle Moses that things in the house were becoming difficult. His wife, Paraska, and his daughter-in-law were constantly fighting. His daughter-in-law had threatened to report the Jews living in the barn to the authorities. Uncle Moses convinced Vasil to tell his family that the Jews had left and that it would be their secret that they stayed. He told Vasil that God would bless him for being so kind. Vasil did not have the heart to turn out the Jewish family to die, so he agreed. He promised to bring some food for Luci when he could. "Every Sunday when I go to church," he added, "I pray for you people."

Aunt Mina was worried. "Vasil only knows about the four of us, and now there will be ten." My father had a solution. "We must dig a bunker in the ground under the straw that can hold the ten of us." Immediately, the men found some tools in the barn and started digging. They worked through the night and dug what looked like a big grave, three metres by three metres square.

Dark and airless. Our positions were organized in such a way that Uncle Moses could lie near the opening so that Vasil would see only him when he came with food. Five people lay on one side and the other five on the opposite side. We lay foot to foot – toes touching. Aunt Mina and Luci lay beside Moses. I lay with my parents. And there was Bubbie Yetta, Shiko and Baruch. And Dr. Nieder.

In these positions we remained. There was no room for standing or moving. When one person had to turn, all of us would have to turn. The deeper we were inside the bunker, the less air we had. There were strict rules for Luci and me. We were kept apart from each other and were not allowed to use our voices to speak. We could only communicate by moving our lips.

Turn. Whisper. Turn.

Sometimes, the adults took pity on us and gave us something important to do. It was our job to wake someone by touching them if they were snoring in their sleep, and that was usually Bubbie Yetta. When we giggled at the strange sounds she made, we were reprimanded with, "Stop laughing and be quiet. The Germans are coming." The word German was enough to make us stop. We knew all too well what that meant. If it wasn't Bubbie who made us laugh it was something else, and then one of the adults would lie on us. Choke us. So we could not breathe.

Turn. Whisper. Turn.

Vasil, of course, had no idea there were ten people hiding in the bunker in his barn. Whenever he could, he brought a little bread or cornmeal called *kolesha*, which Luci liked.

We were all prisoners of the bunker. Feverish and weak. Near the entrance to the bunker stood a tin pail we used as a toilet. We had terrible diarrhea and dysentery. When we passed just one drop of stool the bacteria multiplied and grew until the bucket overflowed. The smell was unbearable.

Late at night, when it was snowing, the men took turns going out to empty the bucket and to search for food. In the winter, food came mainly from pigsties and stables. It was very dangerous to go out and usually only two men went at one time. One stole the food and the other stood on guard. The dogs of the village were the greatest threat. Even though the village was silent and asleep late at night, the barking dogs could easily alert the villagers that someone was about. Each time the men went out, we held our breaths until they returned. My father never even waited for the pigs and cows to finish with their food before he grabbed it from them.

Only Dr. Nieder continued to venture out regularly to meet his girlfriend, Jadwiga, and get the newspaper. They had a special meeting place far away from the farmers' homes and far from our hiding place. By the light of the moon shining on the white snow, he could read how bad the situation was and how far we still were from any hope of freedom.

Uncle Shiko and our friend Baruch found a whole barrel of sauerkraut in a farmer's stable. After the war, Dr. Nieder always said that it was the sauerkraut that had saved our lives. My father and Baruch found a bag of apples in a storage cabin. For water, we melted snow in our hands and drank.

Turn. Whisper. Turn.

~

In the beginning, when my father went out to search for food, he would go see Jozef Beck for news of Uncle Velvel. It wasn't long before he learned that Velvel had died of typhus in the ghetto. My father stood in silence and prayed when he heard. He was overwhelmed with guilt that he had not been able to save his brother from whom he had never been separated before and now would never see again.

As my father walked through the heavy snow, devastated, he could not even feel the terrible cold wind that hit his cheeks. When he came back to the bunker, his hands, feet and face were red and frostbitten. He crawled to his place beside my mother and whispered to her, "There is no more Velvel. He is gone." He whispered, but I heard. My sobs pushed their way out through the silence. In my small world, my uncle had been my special favourite.

Days, nights, weeks and months went on and on. Not even a glimmer that the hell would ever end. Day after day, in a small bunker with so many bodies close together. No light. No sound.

Most of the time it was nearly impossible for me to distinguish between reality and fantasy. Between one day and the next. Between night and day. But there were moments. One night. Everyone was asleep. I felt it penetrate me. Unfamiliar and painful. Something larger than me, forcing its way through me. Someone's toe in my vagina. I began to move slowly, upward a tiny bit, then to the side, but the spaces were too small to hide in. My mother awoke from my fidgeting and was cross that I was not being quiet. She whispered, "Don't move so much. Don't be so selfish. There is not enough room in here for you to be moving so much." I could not tell her what was happening to me.

The sound of Velvel's violin played in my mind. His voice. It helped take me away from the toe and the bunker. I promised myself that I would never forget him as long as I lived. I was seven years old and I didn't know how long that would be.

It became a routine. Our good family friend, Dr. Nieder, continued to abuse me every night after that, often forcing my toes to play with his genitals as well. Over time, I stopped fighting him. He was training me and slowly I began to feel a perverse pleasure from his toes and was somehow pleased to return the same pleasure to him. This ritual continued for the remainder of the time that we were in the bunker.

All my life I have kept this secret. I never told my parents or anyone else. What little innocence I still had at that time he took away from me. It has affected my entire adult life. Sometimes, even today, I cry and mourn the defenseless child that he killed.

By the spring of 1943, the adults were sick of fighting for their miserable existence. But it would still be a very long time before we were free of the horror in the bunker. Dr. Nieder had told us that in February 1943 the ghetto in Kołomyja had been liquidated. We knew there were no more Jews around. It is as difficult now as it was then to understand a world that looked upon this atrocity and allowed it to happen.

~

When spring arrived there were new problems. Food. The men were only able to leave the bunker when it rained because their footsteps would get covered by the mud and the farmers and their dogs stayed indoors. Sometimes the men left at night and it was dawn before they returned. The women worried all night long. Could God have been watching? We never lost anyone.

In the summer, hunting for food was different. The men could go into the fields at night and dig out potatoes, carrots, beets and anything they could put their hands on. I remember that we were often sick with diarrhea and fever. The boredom and fear in the bunker were unbearable and we tried our best to find ways to take our minds off the present and dream of a better life. Aunt Mina would imagine she was a bird and free to fly away. My mother fantasized about food. "When I will be free," she would say, "I would like to have as much bread as I want." "And when I will be free," my aunt would return, "I want to have just boiled potatoes in their skins. As many as I want."

My mother recited poems in German to entertain me. I did not like the sound of the German language and struggled against it. It was strict, harsh and a constant reminder of the Nazis. But it was a language my mother associated with a happy time in her life. It was a language she had learned and cultivated since her early school years, one she relied on now for comfort.

All communication in the bunker was conducted in whispers. I had not used my voice to speak for so long, I had forgotten what it sounded like. Just created words with my lips. We looked like skeletons and were extremely weak. We had not seen daylight for all the time we had been in the bunker. But we pushed the time along, not knowing how much longer we could hold on. How much longer it would take. In the meantime, the war raged and there was no sign of it letting up.

I invented a world of dreams to escape the reality of my life in the bunker. I often brought out Uncle Velvel with his beautiful violin. In my mind, I couldn't separate him from his violin. It was a beautiful violin made in the style of Stradivarius by a German violin maker named Steiner. Velvel was so proud of it and the fact that he owned such an instrument. He had worked a long time to earn enough money to buy the violin from his music teacher. In my mind I replayed the stories Bubbie Frida told me of Velvel taking the horse and carriage, or getting on his bicycle, and going to his violin lessons. In his hands, the violin sang.

I dreamed of bread and butter.

I imagined Zeyde Eli calling me on Saturdays by my Hebrew name, Chai Rachel, asking me to bring him a glass of water. I was there again, on his knee, learning the Hebrew letters. Braiding his beard. Watching him study. Watching the water drip on his white whiskers.

Bubbie Frida's smiling face was constantly on my mind. I saw myself as I repeated the morning and evening prayers with her. As she watched me when I had learned to recite them on my own. As she admired me. As she loved me.

I remembered the peonies and the butterflies and the pony. My dog, Bobby.

I dreamed about the end of the war.

Chapter 13

Soon our second winter in the bunker arrived. It became more and more difficult for the men to go out in search of food. But there was no choice: we still had to survive the winter. The men had no proper clothing and no shoes, so they bundled their feet with rags, though this did not give them much protection against frostbite. The winter of 1943–1944 was our most difficult time. We were at the very limit of our strength and our endurance.

Dr. Nieder had been reading in the paper that the Soviet army was moving closer and pushing the Nazis back. There was a chance that the war would end soon. This gave us a spark of hope. We knew that the next few months would be crucial. Not only would we have to find strength, but we also would need to be even more careful than before. We needed to survive. It was impossible to believe that all ten of us had survived thus far. We were excited and uneasy at the same time. Even if the war ended, what would be waiting for us? Isolated from the world for so long, we did not know what to expect or who we could trust.

In February 1944, we began to hear heavy bombing and the sound of aircraft. It was frighteningly apparent that the front was moving from east to west. I was afraid that a bomb would hit our bunker. Sleep was no longer possible. Vasil Hapiuk was also feeling the pressure. One morning he came to the barn, brought some cornmeal for

Luci and told Moses that the war was coming to an end. The Soviets were pushing the Germans back. He was extremely frightened and wanted them to leave.

"Go," he said to Uncle Moses, "and may God be with the four of you." But there were ten of us. Uncle Moses promised him that he would leave as soon as the next storm came. My father, knowing that we had nowhere to go, began to plan.

On all fours. Hands and knees to the frozen earth. We crawled.

The women, and Luci and I, could not walk. We had been immobile in the bunker for so long that we were unable to stand. Though my father had no strength, he carried me in his arms. So we crawled through the snow to the nearby forest. The pain of the frostbite we suffered was terrible and we trembled and shivered in the bitter cold. It took us the entire night to reach the forest. The men dug a hole and covered it with wood and branches. This would be our new home. We bundled up in blankets and huddled together in the hole under the branches. Now we could hear clearly the airplanes flying overhead and the sound of bombs. We shook, but my father said it was a very good sign.

Hiding in the forest was very difficult, but at least we had fresh air to breathe. The men continued to rummage for food at night in the villages. Again, they competed with the cows and pigs for something to eat. Whatever they could grab, they brought back to us. We were still not using our voices to speak.

Two weeks after Kołomyja was liberated, my father returned from the village one night and told us, "This is it. I saw Russian tanks moving on the main road to Kołomyja.[8] We have to go out to the road and ask the Russian soldiers for help." It was April of 1944 and we had not known until then that Kołomyja had been freed. That night, we crawled on all fours to freedom.

---

8 Kołomyja was liberated by Soviet troops on March 29, 1944.

Chapter 14

It was already dawn when we reached the main road. Tanks were moving heavily, one after another, but we just lay in the ditch by the side of the road hoping that someone would notice us. My father was teaching me the word for "Jewess" in Russian. He kept making me repeat, "Ya Yevreyka." (I am a Jewess.) It was no use though. I could not make my voice speak. No sound came out and I could only move my lips to the words.

When we saw the beginning of daybreak on the horizon, the Soviets still had not noticed us. We were afraid to stay where we were during the day. My father pushed me out of the ditch onto the shoulder of the road. Uncle Moses did the same with Luci. We stayed on the shoulder of the road and practiced in Russian, "Ya Yevreyka." After what seemed like a very long time, one of the soldiers saw us and ordered the tank to stop. Two soldiers got off the tank and picked us up.

I was afraid to tell them I was Jewish. When we escaped from the ghetto, we had ripped off the bands with the Star of David that identified us as Jews. Now I was to tell these soldiers I was Jewish? When the Soviet soldiers picked us up they noticed that there was a whole group of people in the ditch. We did not have to tell them who we were. They understood. They took us to a building in Kołomyja where there was already a group of Jewish survivors who had come out of hiding a little earlier than us. Of the large Jewish population that had lived in Kołomyja and the surrounding area before the war, we were part of only a handful that were left.

"Eat very slowly," the soldier told me, "otherwise you will be very sick." This was our first meal in freedom. The soldiers gave us hot soup, bread, canned meat and canned fruit. It felt like a feast. A meal fit for kings and queens. Now we were under the good care of the Soviet Army. We were given shelter in a building with other survivors from the area and we received medical attention and treatment for our frostbite and swollen, bleeding hands and legs. We were covered in lice and the soldiers gave us clean clothing and poured kerosene over our hair to kill the parasites. Luci and I were treated to hard chocolates. The taste of the chocolate brought back a flood of memories for me. Bubbie Frida. Velvel bringing me chocolates from his trips to Warsaw. I turned to my father and whispered, "Please, Daddy, ask the soldier if he can find Uncle Velvel. He is probably still hiding." My father held me and promised everything would be all right, as I wept in his arms. But the war was not over and there was no real peace yet.

Though the Soviet army had liberated our area, the Germans were still trying to push them back. Kołomyja was under attack. I was petrified of the bombing and low-flying military planes. When the planes flew over our heads, my father screamed, "Lie down on the floor. Quickly! Don't move!" We lay face down with our heads under our cots. We stayed that way for hours, panic in our hearts at the thought of the Germans winning and coming back to finish us off. Finally, a Soviet officer informed us that the Germans were pushing the Soviet army back again and that we would have to leave Kołomyja. We were still very weak and found it difficult to walk. The officer transported us to the train station in his truck. He gave us some canned food, water and chocolate. "This train will take you to the city of Czernowitz, which now belongs to the USSR," he told us.[9] Czernowitz had been

---

9 In March 1944, Czernowitz was occupied by the Red Army and brought fully under the control of the Soviet Union. Many Jews from Galicia, Ukraine and

part of Romania before the war. "There you will be safe."

There were a number of Jewish survivors trying to leave Kołomyja at the same time and we all tried to board the train at once. People became wild, screaming and shoving each other to be the first on the train. Everything was chaotic. Families were separated from each other and people shouted out names into the crowd. It was a horrible scene that confused and frightened me. I remembered how people were taken from the ghetto by train and never came back.

We were on the run again. On the way to Czernowitz, we came to Zuczka, a town where the bridge had been destroyed. The train could not proceed, so we had to get off and walk the rest of the way to Czernowitz. Again, the nightmare of walking in pain and weakness was upon us. We barely made it to the city.

In Czernowitz, the Red Cross immediately took us to the hospital. We were split up into different rooms. For the first time since the war had broken out, I was bathed and slept in a clean bed. Even though I was afraid to be separated from my parents, the nurses were kind and gentle with me. They admired my beautiful long braids, even though they were still full of lice. "Those braids," my father had told them, "have survived the most difficult times of war. They cannot be cut off now." And the nurses promised to take care of my braids.

My family stayed in the hospital to recuperate for several weeks until, in the late spring of 1944, everyone was well enough to leave. Everyone except me, that is. I had a serious problem. Each time I tried to speak, I moved my lips to communicate – but no sound came out. I had to stay in the hospital for speech treatments, but felt I had very little hope of recovery. The tears rolled down my cheeks as my parents hugged me and promised that it would not be long before I was well and could come home. The medical staff tried everything they could to bring out my voice, but nothing seemed to work. The doctors explained to me that the war was over and that there weren't

Bessarabia soon moved to the city as it was relatively safe compared to neighbouring areas where German-Soviet battles continued.

any Germans around. I nodded my head to show that I understood what they were saying, but I remained silent. I tried my best to speak. I wanted so badly to speak, to be able to answer their questions, and I was so frustrated and ashamed of my inability to help myself. I was truly afraid that I would remain speechless for the rest of my life.

The doctors continued their work every day, but there was no progress. Finally, they decided to use reverse psychology to shock me into speaking. Two doctors entered my room and stopped near the window. One of the doctors looked out and shouted, "The Germans are back. They are here." When I heard that, I jumped out of my bed and gave a long, petrified scream. I tried to run out of the room, screaming, "NO! NO! NO!" One of the doctors rushed to me and, holding me close, whispered softly, "Don't be afraid. It's all right. The Germans are far away from here. You are safe."

I did not know who to believe at first, but I saw that the doctors were not afraid or running for their lives to hide. Maybe it really was safe. When the doctors finally calmed me down, we began to speak. This was the first conversation I had had in several years. My voice had finally come back to me.

Part Three:
Post-war Poland

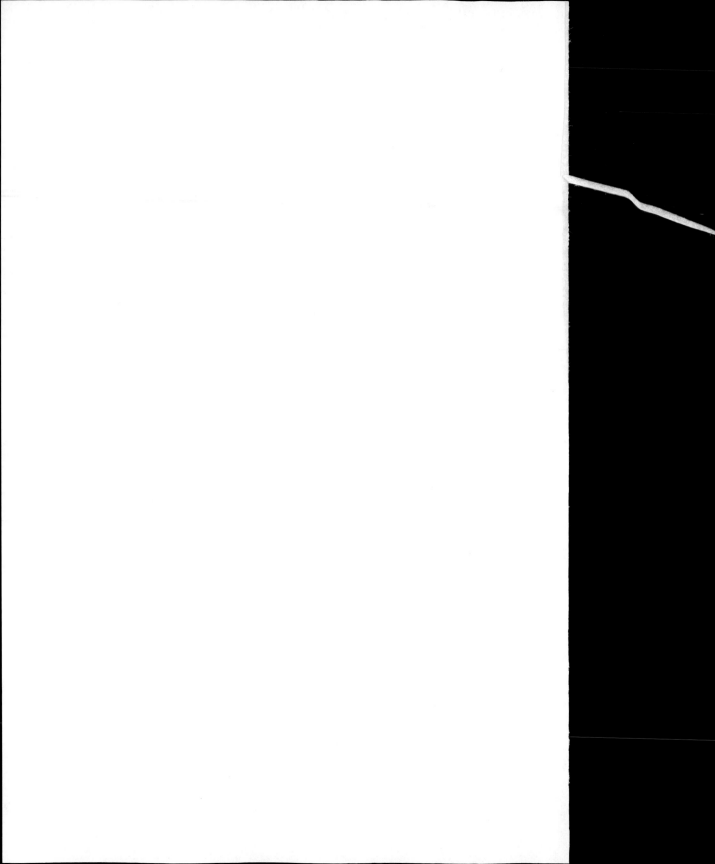

Chapter 15

And so life began again.

The Soviet authorities had assigned a small apartment to my parents in Czernowitz and, in the autumn of 1944, they were working on a farm in the village of Kamionka, near Czernowitz. My father worked as a gardener and my mother as the cook on what was called a *kolkhoz*, or collective farm.

I was learning to be happy.

At last, after years of hiding, I was free.[10] I was free to live, to breathe fresh air, to be equal to other children. Most of all, I was grateful that both my parents had survived and could take care of me. The love, care and devotion that I had known as a small child in Turka now returned. It became possible to believe that the love I had felt from Bubbie Frida, Zeyde Eli and Uncle Velvel was being passed down to me through my parents. It made me stronger.

I was nine years old. My mother insisted that I use the name Rose outside of our home. She told me that with a name like Rose, no one would think I was Jewish and it would be easier for me to fit in with

---

10 Although the war continued in other parts of Europe until May 1945, hostilities ceased in Czernowitz when the Soviet Union took control in March 1944, and in the surrounding areas during the summer of 1944.

other children. She also felt that I would be safer, because there was still a great deal of antisemitism around us.[11]

Luci and I were enrolled in a Russian school. It was the first time in my life that I attended school. I did not know even one letter of the Russian alphabet. I tried to remember the Hebrew letters my zeyde had taught me once, but nothing looked familiar. I had no idea what the teacher was saying or teaching. I just sat and thought about other things. I knew I had a lot of making up to do for all those lost years, but I also wanted to play. It was a difficult time for me, recuperating from the traumas of the past and trying to grasp the meaning of a normal life.

I still remember the first pair of shoes my father bought me when he had earned enough money. I tried on several pairs in the shop and my father kept asking me which ones felt the most comfortable. I told him that I would have to dance in them first to know which were the best. My father looked at me in disbelief. I had always been so shy and now I wanted to dance – in the shop, in the presence of strangers. I quickly put on a pair of shoes and started humming, dancing around the room to the Russian dance *Kozaczok*. My father, beaming, agreed that the shoes I had on were perfect for me. I could not remember the last time I had worn shoes. I was the happiest girl in the whole world.

Even at this innocent moment of happiness, the memory of the Germans taking our shoes away when we first arrived in the ghetto flooded my mind. "Why would they have done that?" I asked myself. "So we could not run fast enough to escape," I answered.

As we walked home from the shoe shop, my new shoes on my feet, it began to rain. I immediately took off my shoes and walked bare-

---

11 Jewish Holocaust survivors returning to their hometowns in Poland and other Eastern-European countries after the war often experienced widespread hostility at the hands of their neighbours, including, in some extreme cases, murder. See Jan T. Gross, *Fear: Anti-Semitism in Poland after Auschwitz* (New York: Random House, 2006).

foot. These shoes were so precious to me that I wanted to make sure that the rain did not ruin them. I was more concerned for them than for my own tortured feet. This concern continued for about a year after the war. Whenever it rained or snowed I would walk barefoot, cradling my shoes in my arms.

Chapter 16

In the fall of 1944, when we were in Czernowitz, word had begun to spread that Soviet authorities were forcibly recruiting young men and women to work in Siberia. Only families who were expecting babies were exempt. On July 14, 1945, I came home from a friend's house to find that my mother was not home. I kept knocking at our door, but the door was locked and no one answered. Our neighbour heard me and opened her door. "Come in, Rachel," she said, "your parents have a surprise for you. You have a baby sister. Wait here with me until your father comes to pick you up." A baby sister! I was shocked. I had not been told that my mother was expecting a baby.

I stood with my father outside the hospital and the nurse showed us the baby through a window. I looked down at the tiny face and began to feel love for her. I was proud and felt very lucky to have a beautiful baby sister. She was blond, with curly hair and big blue eyes, just like Bubbie Frida, for whom she had been named. I loved being allowed to take care of her and tried to help my mother as much as possible.

In July 1945, with the war completely over, my father decided to move our family back to Kołomyja. I did not like this decision. Kołomyja brought back horrible memories of the ghetto and the loss of Uncle Velvel, Bubbie Frida and Zeyde Eli. Nevertheless, my father was determined to return to familiar surroundings.

Although we had only been there for about a year, I missed Czernowitz terribly when we left. I missed Luci. Again, I relied on my
memories to see me through. I remembered all the adventures we
had together; how we had contracted scarlet fever together and were
kept in the same bed during the illness. As soon as my mother would
leave the room, we would take turns hanging off the door and swinging from it. We would spend the whole day swinging on the wooden
door, not resting.

I recalled staying in bed with my mother on the days when Bubbie Yetta washed our only set of clothing. I remembered the clothing
I had worn in the war, in shreds, full of lice and not worth saving.
My mother had destroyed them. She did not want reminders of the
nightmare we had lived. Aunt Mina kept Luci's as a memento.

Most of all, I missed going to the cinema with Luci. We went almost every day in Czernowitz. If our parents did not want to give
us money, we tried to frighten them and told them we would report
their cruelty to the police. That always seemed to work. Inside the
cinema, we would run to sit in the front row. When the lights were
turned down before the movie started, Luci and I would huddle together and hold hands, fighting our fear of the dark, waiting for the
first flickers of light on the screen.

When we arrived in Kołomyja, the Soviet authorities assigned a
small house to us – Zamkowa Street, No. 6 – and we began to put
our lives together. My father looked for ways to make money and
embarked on a small business repairing watches for Soviet soldiers.
He was not a watchmaker, but he would play around with the mech-
anisms and somehow make the watches work again. After a short
time, he put a sign in our window saying, "Watch Repair" and people
in the city began bringing him their watches. My father was happy.
He was able to support his family and was rebuilding his life.

Shortly after we settled into our new home, many Jewish families who had lived in Kołomyja before the war and had survived by
escaping to the USSR returned to look for their loved ones. From

our own community, we were among the very few who had survived the German occupation. One of those who returned was a young woman, Regina Dankner. She had lived in Kołomyja before the war with her parents and sister, but she had escaped to the Soviet Union alone. None of her family had survived. Uncle Shiko remembered her. She was very pretty with thick black braids and dimples on both cheeks. Shiko and Regina were a perfect match and were very quickly married.

Before the war, Kołomyja had belonged to Poland. After the war, the borders had changed and Kołomyja became part of the USSR. My father discovered that since we were Polish citizens before the war, we had the choice to return to Poland or remain in the USSR and apply for citizenship. The decision was made to leave Kołomyja and move west into Poland. Everyone who had survived the Holocaust with us in the bunker decided to go to Poland, as did my new aunt, Regina.

~

It was the winter of 1946. We owned practically nothing, so it was very easy to pack. But my father had not forgotten what Velvel had told him in the ghetto. Velvel said he had buried his violin near our house in Turka just before the Germans forced us from our home. Now, before we left, my father and Uncle Shiko knew they had to go and find the violin.

One clear night, they walked out to the main road leading to the village of Turka. They were lucky enough to be picked up by a military truck; the driver agreed to take them to their destination. As they approached their childhood home, they both began to shake and their hearts beat wildly. My father knew approximately where the violin had been buried and went straight to the side of the house near the fence where the old walnut tree was still standing. They began to dig. Finally, under the fence, they found it. Holding his breath, my father picked up the kilim-wrapped violin and looked at his brother. Together, they ran to the main road and made their way back to

Kołomyja. We greeted them with great relief and much excitement when they arrived. My father walked into the living room, put the kilim-wrapped violin on a chair and, choking back the tears, said, "This is all we have left of Velvel." Now the emotions he had managed to hold in until he reached home burst forth, and he broke down and wept. Velvel's final wish had been fulfilled. We unwrapped the kilim and opened the violin case for the first time.

The case and the bow were almost rotten, but the violin itself was damaged in only one tiny spot. As my father turned the precious instrument in his hands, we could clearly see the word Steiner written on the neck. Along with the violin, Velvel had put several baby pictures of me and a few photos of other people in the case. There was a picture of my mother and me when I was six months old and a picture of Bubbie Yetta sitting with me on the grass in Bubbie Frida's garden. There was a picture of my father, Uncle Moses and me when I was a year old, and one of Aunt Mina, her two cousins and me when I was four years old. There was a picture of Uncle Velvel wearing his beautiful, colourful embroidered shirt. Looking at the pictures of Velvel, everyone was amazed at how much I had grown to resemble him. It made me proud to look like him.

At the bottom of the stack there was one last photo. A picture of Velvel's cousin Minka and beside her, a young girl. Dark. Blond. Pretty. A friend? Both of them laughing and holding hands.

Chapter 17

It was a difficult, week-long journey from Kołomyja into Poland. We travelled, crowded together on a cargo train with other survivors going home. The inside of the train was a shock to me and looked more suitable for farm animals than for humans. There were big sliding doors but no windows. At each end of the car, on the floor, were kerosene lamps that helped to light the space when the door was closed. The air in the train car was dense with cigarette smoke, and only when the train stopped at each station would the door be slid wide open to let in fresh air and the light of day. It was at these times that passengers could get out to relieve themselves and wash their hands and faces. Children, however, were not allowed to leave the train in case they wandered off, so I used the chamber pot, which my father emptied at each stop. Everywhere, the floor was littered with mattresses and blankets on which we sat and lay down to sleep. Each family was responsible for themselves. My father, being a very practical man, had brought along canned food. We had canned meat, sardines, juices, dark rye bread and two large containers of drinking water, which we used sparingly.

The days dragged by. Most of the time on the train, Luci and I played with my little sister, Frida. We invented games to entertain and distract her, blowing air onto her soft little cheeks whenever she cried. Luci, Frida and I were an alliance in the way Luci and I had been before Frida was born. Although Frida was my sister, it was always the three of us. Cousins. Sisters. Friends.

At other times, I occupied myself by observing the people around me. I realized during these observations that the people with whom we were sharing the train were very unusual. There was a wild little girl, a bit younger than I, who was always jumping around and screaming to be left alone in the corner. I will never forget how she looked. She had long, thick black hair that covered her face and hands. Her parents explained that they had given her to a Ukrainian peasant family at the beginning of the war and that they themselves had survived hiding in the forests and villages. After the war, they returned to reclaim their daughter to find that she did not remember them and resisted their attempts to explain who they were. Nothing helped and they finally had to use force to remove her from the Ukrainian family.

There was also a very pretty sixteen-year-old girl whom Luci and I greatly admired. Sonia had a beautiful round face with dimples in her cheeks, big brown eyes and a small straight nose. Her thick brown hair curled gently around her shoulders. Best of all, I loved her smile that set off her beautiful small teeth. Sonia told us she had no family and had survived the Nazis alone. She soon became the centre of attention of the whole group in our car and, in particular, of a young man travelling with his uncle, who began showering her with compliments and openly hugging and kissing her. He announced that he had fallen madly in love with her and asked for her hand in marriage. She agreed at once. How, I wondered, could she accept a stranger's proposal? Two days later an older man married them on the train, as Luci and I stood watching excitedly. Now she would have someone to care for her and she wouldn't have to be alone in the world.

The strangest of all those in the train was an old man who sat next to me. He had taken a liking to me and kept calling me over to sit on his lap. He made me very uneasy and something told me not to go near him. He was very skinny and had a terrible congestive cough. Whenever he had a coughing spell, he spit up a pile of sputum on the floor and it made me sick to watch. I was angry that he would not leave me alone and wished my parents were paying more attention to what was happening. Finally, reluctantly, feeling obliged to be polite, I sat beside him while he talked to me, occasionally hugging me.

At last we arrived in the city of Bytom in an area of Poland called Upper Silesia. My father registered with authorities from the Jewish community who were working to resettle returning survivors and refugees. We were given an apartment in a tall, dark, grey building on Powstańców Street. Shiko and Regina also moved into our building, two floors below us. Luci's family moved into an apartment building further down the street.

Within a few days of our arrival in Bytom, I became very ill. I began coughing badly, could not catch my breath, and developed a high fever. My parents gave me aspirin, but it did not help. The cough persisted and became very painful. Shiko, who worked as a doctor's aide, tried to treat me with *banki*. This treatment consisted of soaking a piece of cotton in alcohol and inserting it through the narrow opening of small round glass jar. The cotton was then lit and the glass jar immediately applied to the back, where the flame died as the seal did not allow oxygen to enter. This created a vacuum that was thought to suck out the poisons through the skin. Several *banki* were applied to my back at the same time. This procedure was painful and left my skin swollen, red and hot.

I could not attend school and was in bed constantly. I had no appetite. I lost weight and became malnourished. The *banki* were not helping and my family sat around my bed crying and praying. My family was not sure if I would survive. Through my fever and illness I could hear them saying, "After all she has been through and has survived, we are not going to lose her now."

My father was finally able to find a Jewish doctor, Dr. Tuszkiewicz, who was a lung specialist. I was taken to his clinic. He was kind and friendly as he checked my lungs and took x-rays and blood tests. He promised that he would help me. To my father, however, he spoke very seriously. I was afraid that he was telling him that there was no cure for me. After speaking to my father for a while, he told me he would be working on my case with another Jewish doctor, Dr. Brzeski. Together, the two doctors came to the same diagnosis: tuberculosis. The man on the train had infected me; my father later found out that he died two months after our trip together.

I needed daily intra-muscular injections in my thighs, which were given to me by Dr. Brzeski personally. They were terribly painful. My father usually took me, but when he had to go out of town on business, he asked Aunt Mina to take me. She would walk with me to the doctor's office holding my hand the whole time. On the way, we always passed a bakery and Aunt Mina would say, "If you promise to behave and take the needles like a grownup girl, I will buy you any pastry you choose on the way home." Of course, I promised. Each day after my difficult visit to the doctor, Aunt Mina took me into the bakery where I asked for a cream custard pastry called a napoleon. It smelled so good and gave me such comfort as I held it in my hands.

Almost as bad as the needles was the fact that I had to be isolated from the rest of the family, especially from Frida and my mother. My mother was very occupied with Frida and worried about her becoming infected. It upset me that I could not be close to my mother and that she did not lie down beside me and tell me stories as she used to in the bunker. I missed her hugging me and was hurt by the fact that she never came with me for my needles. When I asked her to come instead of Aunt Mina, she told me, "I cannot leave Frida. You will be all right." My father, on the other hand, was very caring during my illness and was not afraid of getting infected. He would lie down next to me in bed and cuddle with me, comforting me with stories. He insisted that my mother prepare a concoction of raw egg yolk and sugar called a *gogl-mogl* every day. He believed that this would relieve my throat, raw from the constant coughing. Every day he would ask her, "Sara, did you make Rachel her special drink today? It wouldn't hurt even if she had it a few times a day."

During that time, my father and Shiko tried to find a way to make a living. My father had always been very resourceful and they travelled back to Kołomyja several times to buy goods such as leather purses, perfumes, socks, cigarettes and a variety of canned foods that they would then bring back for Aunt Regina to sell in the marketplace. On one occasion, my father returned from one of these trips with a raincoat he had bought especially for me. I had never owned a raincoat before. How excited I was by this tiny black-and-white checkered coat. I waited impatiently every day for the rain. One night, after I was already in bed, our friend and neighbour, Baruch, came to visit. He was standing at the door, soaked to the bone, and said to my mother, "What a downpour! There isn't a dry thread on my body." I immediately jumped out of bed and reached for my raincoat. I begged Baruch to come downstairs with me and stand in the building entrance so that I could walk in the rain. What a wonderful man! He stood in the doorway for over an hour as I marched back and forth on the sidewalk in my new raincoat.

When I finally recovered from my illness, the two doctors who had cared for me advised my father that the climate in Upper Silesia was very bad for people with lung problems. Bytom was a coal-mining city and the charcoal dust in the air was deadly for my lungs. They suggested that we move as soon as possible. Dr. Brzeski promised he would visit us often to monitor my health and provide any further advice.

My father decided we would settle in Wrocław, a large city with many Jews and a good school. He quickly found a nice furnished apartment and a delicatessen nearby that he and Shiko could run together. It was 1947. I was twelve years old and my sister, Frida, was two years old. Our family, Shiko's family, Mina's family and our dear friend Baruch prepared to move yet again.

Chapter 18

Wrocław had been a part of Germany before the war, when it was called Breslau. It was a dreary place, with the occasional dark, grey building still standing amid the ruins of war. Our apartment had belonged to a German family before the war who had fled Poland afterward.[12] It was nicely furnished. The dining room had a huge oak table surrounded by ten leather-covered chairs and two matching armchairs. The china cabinet and hutches were filled with crystal and in the centre of the cabinet was a mirror. My parents had a white antique French-provincial bedroom set and Uncle Shiko and Aunt Regina had bedroom furniture made of cherry wood.

The living room was very cozy. It had a white-coloured brick fireplace in the corner near the entrance. An antique desk was positioned between the two large windows facing the street. A small grandfather clock hung over the desk on the wall. Along the wall on the other side of the room there was a bookcase. My mother had a photographer enlarge a photo of Velvel that we found in the violin case, and she hung it in the living room. A few years later, a coloured portrait taken

---

12 After World War II, Wrocław was ceded to Poland and the German population of the city was officially transferred to Germany. It was replaced with a Polish population from the former Polish city Lvov, which in turn was ceded to the Soviet Union.

of me when I was fifteen years old was placed under the portrait of Velvel on the wall.

In the mornings, my father went to the marketplace. It was a gathering place for people to discuss politics, exchange ideas and look for missing friends and relatives. One morning, my father happened upon Jozef and Rozalia Beck, whom he discovered were living on a farm in the village of Lutynia near Wrocław. He brought them back to our house. Finally, he had the chance to repay Jozef and Rozalia for all they had sacrificed for us during the war. He offered to help Jozef buy some farm equipment that he badly needed. We continued to see them often; they came to visit us in the city and we frequently visited them on the farm. Our families, who had forged an extraordinary relationship during extraordinary times, were now very close again and our deep and caring friendship continued for a long time.

My father also discovered that Dr. Nieder and Jadwiga, now married, were living in Wrocław. He was the man who had abused me in the bunker. I had tried to push what he did to me out of my mind, but it was extremely difficult as my parents saw him frequently. When he came to our house to visit, he was very affectionate with me and would find every opportunity to compliment me and treat me as if I were somehow more important to him than the others. I shrank at his touch. Tried to stay away. In my heart, I could never forgive him for the damage he had done to me at such a horrific time and tender stage of my childhood.

When we arrived in Wrocław, it was late fall and the school year had already begun. One morning, Aunt Mina dropped by with Luci and announced that she was enrolling Luci at the Shalom Aleichem Jewish School. "If you want," Aunt Mina said, "I could take Rachel along too and register her at the school." "Good," my mother replied, "sign up Rachel too. I can't leave the baby alone."

It was very difficult to be without my mother on the first day of school. I was nervous about meeting the new teachers and children but, as always, my mother had her ready excuse – Frida. It was painful to feel as though I was unimportant to her. I was beginning to see a pattern. Any issue that had to do directly with me was taken care of by my father or, if he was not available, Aunt Mina. How I envied Luci that first day as we walked to school. Her mother cared about her.

When we arrived at the school for registration, we met the principal, Mr. Tencer. Aunt Mina explained to him how Luci and I had lost years during the war and that we did not know the alphabet and would need a lot of help catching up to our appropriate grade level. Mr. Tencer decided to put Luci and me in Grade 3, even though he felt we should be in Grade 1. He did not want us to feel uncomfortable with smaller children. He told us that there were other students in the school who had survived the war in Russia and that they were also academically delayed. He took both of us to our classroom. Luci went happily to her seat, but I remained standing at the door. The principal turned to me and asked me to join the class, telling me that very soon I would make a lot of new friends. I was very upset. I was a year older than Luci and we would be in the same grade.

I did not move.

I would not set foot in that class. Realizing that something was very wrong, Mr. Tencer took me out to the corridor. Talking to me very gently, he said, "Rachel, why don't you want to be in the same class as your cousin Luci?" I answered, shyly, "I am a year older than she is and I should be in a higher grade." Smiling, he bent down and patted my shoulder. "You are right, Rachel. What do you think about Grade 4?" I nodded my head and without hesitation followed him into the Grade 4 class.

~

Even though it was a difficult first day, I knew that an exciting new world was opening up for me. I soon felt very comfortable at the school, being with other Jewish children and being able to use my Jewish name, Rachel. But the horror of the world I had known in the ghetto and the bunker still lived inside me.

It took me an hour and a half to get to and from school each day. It was a one-and-a-half-kilometre-long walk to the streetcar from home, a thirty-minute streetcar ride to my first transfer, another thirty-minute streetcar ride after that, and another one-and-a-half-kilometre-long walk past rubble and a cemetery.

We lived on Dworcowa Street, near the main train station of the city. That street, like so many others, had been destroyed by the war. The school, on Grabiszyńska Street, was also in a section of the city that had been devastated by the bombing. Every day on the way to school I passed the reminders of war. Ruins of bombed-out buildings. Bullet-ridden walls in the buildings that remained standing. Tombstones. Too many memories flooded my mind.

Before long, I settled into my new life at school. During class one afternoon, the principal came into our class and introduced a new boy. A boy with blue eyes and straight blond hair combed with a part on the side. On first sight, this boy made me very nervous. During the break he told us that his father was Jewish and that he had a German mother. I was shocked. How could our Jewish school have accepted him? My heart began to pound and I could feel an uncontrollable rage building in my chest. "He's a German! He killed my family!" I screamed. "He murdered my uncle Velvel and all the children in the ghetto. I don't want him in my class." I strained to kick him, but some of the other children held me back. Every child in our class felt hatred and fear when they heard the word "German." Every one of them understood what was happening to me. Some of the bigger boys in the class pounced on him and beat the new boy very badly that day. We injured and humiliated him. He ran out of the class and never came back.

I graduated that year with excellent marks. The teachers were very proud of my accomplishments, but I was not satisfied. Still one grade behind my age group, I was determined to skip another year. Again, the principal was very understanding and told me to study during summer vacation. If I passed the test in September, he said he would allow me to skip Grade 5 and go to Grade 6. Throughout the summer my father studied with me. He bought me *A Thousand and One Stories* by the Brothers Grimm and I read stories aloud to him each night in Polish, quickly becoming fluent. I worked hard to excel in math, which was my favourite subject. Tirelessly, he practiced writing and reading in Yiddish with me. Suddenly, summer turned into fall. I took the exam and passed. Grade 6. I was the youngest in the class.

Chapter 19

My father had great expectations for me. It was his mission in life to see me excel at everything. "Rachel," he said to me one morning, "I want you to take violin lessons. Velvel left the violin for you. It is his legacy and it would mean a great deal to me if you would learn to play it just like he did." I looked at my father in surprise. "But I don't like the violin and don't want to play it." I could see that I had disappointed him. "Which instrument would you like to play, then?" he asked softly. I hated disappointing him. "The piano," I answered quickly. "Fine," he replied. "Let's make a deal. I will get you a piano, but you will also learn to play the violin. Velvel was a very talented violinist. I believe that you can be as well. What do you say, my diamond?"

I was shocked by this sudden turn of events. I had to think it over. I finally decided that it was better to play both instruments than to play none at all. Before long, my father had me signed up at the Hubert Music Conservatory and three men delivered a beautiful, shiny, black grand piano to our apartment.

The lessons at the conservatory soon became a huge part of my life. I took violin lessons with Mr. Bindes twice a week, followed immediately by piano lessons with Mrs. Sneider. Soon more subjects were added to the instrument instruction: theory, rhythm, history of music and, soon after, much more. Between music lessons and school, I hardly had time for anything else. Sometimes I forgot that I was still a child.

I began to play concerts for company at home. My father's eyes would well up with tears each time I played. On Shabbat, he would accompany me by singing songs from the Torah. He expected nothing less than outstanding performances from me and would become quite unhappy if I received a bad grade in school or did poorly at a recital. My mother, on the other hand, was strangely cool to my achievements. When I played for company she would interrupt, starting conversations almost deliberately to distract my audience. Angrily, I would sometimes stop playing altogether and leave the room.

It wasn't only with regard to my music that my mother and I had problems. Frida was becoming an issue. In the rare moments when I found some time to spend with friends, my mother would insist I take care of Frida. Sometimes I brought her with me to play with friends in our neighbourhood. Once, I was distracted for a moment and she wandered off. My mother flew into a panicked rage. Crying and screaming, she began to comb the streets looking for Frida. I attempted to help in her search but she chased me away, yelling, "If we don't find her, you don't have to bother coming home ever again. Just stay away from us." I was devastated.

Incidents like this and others caused a great deal of bitterness between my mother and me. We argued constantly. Many nights I went to bed without eating dinner just to avoid her tirades. Her complaints hurt and bewildered me. My father would quietly come to see me when he returned from work. "Please come with me to the kitchen," he would say. "I bought some dry salami and fresh rolls. Your favourites. We could have a bite together. You know that I don't like to eat alone." His soft voice and tender concern made me feel protected and loved. I trusted what he felt for me.

~

On New Year's Day 1949, my cousin Eli Milbauer was born. Uncle Shiko and Aunt Regina named their firstborn son after Zeyde Eli. Finally, the two dearest people in the world to me had been renamed in a new generation. Again, I started to hear the names Eli and Frida around me and it was a comfort like no other.

I continued to do well at the music conservatory and joined the string band, where I played second violin. Proudly, my father attended all the recitals. I was also making very good progress with my piano lessons and performed at recitals, often getting standing ovations and loud applause from the crowds. Occasionally, I travelled to various venues to perform at special concerts and benefits. I was thrilled to receive so much attention. But secretly, my wish was to play the Gypsy music I remembered so fondly from my childhood years. I told my teachers, but they felt that it was too soon for me to be learning the Hungarian czardas and insisted I needed a lot more practice.

When I turned fifteen I finally had my chance. There was a competition among the different schools for the best artistic performance. Rita Mirman was not a student in my class, but she did go to my school. She was around my age and was a very talented ballerina. Beautiful, with long black hair and black eyes, she reminded me of the young Gypsy girls of my childhood. Rita approached me when the competition was announced and asked if I could play a czardas at the competition. "If you play then I will dance a Gypsy dance." She had read my mind. Immediately, I bought the sheet music for the czardas by the Hungarian composer Monti and told my piano teacher that she would have to help me practice this piece of music, which she did, to perfection. Rita and I practiced and dreamed of the competition. The day of the competition arrived. We presented our program and won first prize. After that we became almost famous in our town and were invited to perform our special program on many occasions.

After each performance, I would lie in bed with my eyes closed and relive the vision of Rita dancing in her Gypsy costume, a tambourine in her hand, and me at the piano playing the czardas. Music took me to another world – a world that reminded me of the Gypsies on our farm, dancing around the fire in their colourful outfits, the sound of their music filling the air.

My father always tried to provide Frida and me with the things we needed or wanted, even during those difficult times in Wrocław. People had to stand in line for hours to buy clothing and shoes and in the end had to be content with the wrong sizes and colours. But my father commissioned a shoemaker and a tailor to make shoes and clothing especially for Frida and me. Grey for Frida, navy for me. A brocade Chinese housecoat had caught my fancy. He managed to find the perfect fabric. The tailor made me the most beautiful turquoise and gold housecoat, which I still have to this day. For my fifteenth birthday my father bought me a brand-new bicycle.

Chapter 20

By 1951 I was in Grade 9 and my relationship with Luci had changed. We rarely met anymore, only running into each other at school during breaks or at the Saturday-night dances. As we grew older, we lost touch and no longer had common interests or mutual friends. Being involved with music and studies left me very little time for socializing. Besides, new relationships were taking the place of old ones. At that time, my teacher had placed the class into small study groups. Each group consisted of three students who lived near each other. My group consisted of two boys, Leon, who was Rita Mirman's brother, a boy named Peter and myself. Our little trio reminded me of my old childhood friends the Mecios in Turka. The three of us really enjoyed working together and agreed to meet every day at my house between seven and nine o'clock in the evening.

After our first few study sessions, I could tell that Peter liked the warm atmosphere of our apartment and felt at home there. He would always mention how different his home was and that while he was with me he didn't want to even think about his house. I noticed that he began paying more attention to me at school. He would gently tug at my braids and after school he would ask me to join him and his friends in a game of basketball or volleyball. Peter and I found out very quickly that we had a lot in common. We even had the same violin teacher.

Peter and I began spending time together and one evening, as we were coming home from an Italian movie starring Sophia Loren, Peter stopped and kissed me passionately. He wanted me to be his girlfriend. With my heart beating wildly, I accepted without a second thought. I had been dreaming of just that. After that night, when our little trio finished our homework, Leon would leave and Peter would stay behind. We would practice different ways of kissing, copying the movie stars. Finally, I had a true friend. I was in love for the first time in my life.

~

In the spring of 1951, I was sixteen years old and my mother was forty-four. I returned from school one afternoon to find my father standing by the living room window praying. My mother was in bed, unconscious. My father quietly told me that he had called the medical clinic and that the doctor had been to see her. The doctor had taken her blood and urine samples with him for testing, assuring my father that she was not in a serious situation. But my mother was now unconscious and I was petrified.

With very few choices, my father sent me to search for Dr. Nieder. Panic-stricken, I ran to the streetcar. From the streetcar, I saw Dr. Nieder walking down the street. I jumped off the moving streetcar and, with cars speeding by me and my legs like rubber, I rolled to the side of the road and landed directly at his feet. He looked down at me in shock. I could not speak and as he began to help me up, I could do nothing but wail and cry. I managed to articulate that my mother was sick and that he needed to come to see her right away.

When we arrived, Dr. Nieder sniffed the air and said, anxiously, "I smell acetone." He immediately called an ambulance and my mother was taken to the hospital where Dr. Nieder was the director. Tests showed that my mother had diabetes and that she was in a ketone-induced coma, which, if left untreated, would have led to certain death. She stayed in a coma for three weeks. While Aunt Mina looked after Frida, my mother remained in the hospital hooked up to life-support systems. Everything from nourishment to insulin was pumped through her veins. We had very little hope for her recovery. I sat by her side, day after day, watching her pale face and dry, cold skin for any sign of life. After three long weeks, she miraculously regained consciousness.

When my mother was released from the hospital, my father arranged a vacation for Aunt Regina, her son, Eli, my cousin Luci, Frida and me. This would give my mother time alone to recuperate. Jastarnia, on the Baltic Sea, was beautiful. Dark purple and burgundy pansies fluttered in the breeze. Other vacationers strolled by, sunburned, relaxed and happy. The bay was always calm and warm and the sea beyond, wild and strong. As the oldest, I took charge of Luci and Frida, with whom I shared a room. Aunt Regina took care of Eli in another room.

The sea was just across from our hotel and we spent our mornings tanning, jumping in the waves of the Baltic and making new friends. In the afternoons Aunt Regina would take Frida and Eli for a walk along the avenue, leaving Luci and me free to read our books while sitting on the benches along the boardwalk. Every morning we came down to the bright, sunny dining room to eat and in the evenings we listened to music. It was unforgettable. But I missed Peter and wrote him many letters.

We came home to find the apartment newly painted and bright. My mother, relaxed and recovered, sat by the window and embroidered new curtains for the kitchen. Peter came to see me the first evening we were back and, as we strolled in the evening light, he told me about his summer vacation at camp and I told him about the sea. We had missed each other. Summer was ending. We returned to school and our study group resumed its regular meetings.

Peter and I were able to share some of our deepest fears with each other. I often told him about my fear of the darkness and how I imagined the Germans chasing me. "Just check behind you," he would tell me softly. "You'll see, sweet Rachel, they're not chasing you anymore." He told me about his life at home, his stepfather and the little brother he was expected to care for all the time. He confided to me that, although they had never met me, his stepfather liked me very much, but his mother did not. She believed that Peter should not bother with a girl who was obviously too small to produce any children. Angrily, I shouted, "But your mother has never seen me and does not even know me! How can she judge me so harshly?" Peter had no answer to that. "But I still love you," was all he could say.

My size had touched a nerve. This was also a great concern for my father. All the females in my family were of medium height, but I remained the shortest at 147 centimetres. I was the same height that I had been at age ten, just after the war. I was not really troubled by my height. At school, there were a few girls who were my height and with my friends I did not feel uncomfortable. My father, however, took it so seriously that he brought me to see an endocrinologist, Professor Ber, who lived in Lodz. When he heard my story of the war years he told us that he believed my growth had been stunted by the lack of sunlight I had endured lying cramped in the bunker for so long. The years of starvation had not helped.

Professor Ber took x-rays of my bones, many blood tests and we made another appointment. My father was hopeful and happy that soon I would grow taller. For the follow-up appointment, my father and I took an airplane. It was my first time flying and I had to take time off from school for the trip. Professor Ber was hopeful as the test results showed that my bones still had a good chance of growing. He prescribed various hormones for me to take, some in the form of needles and some in the form of tablets. We were encouraged. I continued to see Professor Ber periodically until I turned eighteen, but I grew very little. Professor Ber's last words to me were, "You are a beautiful girl. One day your husband will carry you proudly in his arms."

Chapter 21

In 1953, Stalin died. His death announcement came while I was in school and the reaction was quite emotional. We were upset and saddened by Stalin's death.[13] I was eighteen and it was our last year of high school. Peter, Leon and I had worked very hard and had accomplished a great deal, passing all our exams – written and oral – with excellent marks. We were now on our way to higher education.

Being accepted to a university in the communist system meant having to conform to special requirements and conditions. The most important of these was belonging to a farming or working-class family. Since my parents and grandparents had come from a village and had been farmers, this was not a problem for me. Another requirement was far more difficult. Parents, or the students applying, had to be members of the Communist Party. My father had consistently resisted joining the Communists. He wanted to remain politically neutral and so did the rest of my family. The final criterion was academic. I was lucky that my farming roots and my good marks were enough to gain me admittance to the Wrocław Medical Academy.

---

13 At the time, many people were unaware of the extent of Stalin's own murderous policies. Many Jews in Poland viewed him as the leader of the country that liberated them and saved them from death at Hitler's hands.

Peter applied to the Military School of Technology in Warsaw and Leon planned to attend the college in our city. Peter was the only one of us who would be leaving.

My parents threw me a surprise graduation party, inviting all of my friends and many of their friends as well. Dr. Nieder was there. He approached me during the celebration, handed me a gift and whispered in my ear, "This silver compact is for you. Now that you are mature you will be allowed to put powder on your face." He hugged me and kissed my cheek. I recoiled. He left me speechless and in shock, although I would have liked to tell him, "You took care of my maturity in the bunker when I was seven."

When I looked at my parents' faces I knew they were proud of me and I felt very special. None of my friends' parents had made such a fuss for their children's graduations. My father, of course, asked me to play the violin and the piano for our guests. I was happy to do anything for him and to bask in his affection and pride.

When I had begun my studies at the Jewish school, there were twenty-five or thirty children in each classroom. During my years there, many immigrated to Israel and fewer and fewer children remained in the classes. By 1953, when I graduated high school, there were only eight students in my graduating class. We were all very close then and remain so to this day.

During the summer of 1953, my mother, Frida and I took a holiday in Międzyzdroje, a resort on the Baltic Sea. My father now worked in Wrocław as a manager in a department store. By the time fall came, I had mastered my mother's daily insulin injections. She always complimented me on my steady hands. Strangely, the fact that she let me give her the injections made me feel good and reinforced my desire to become a doctor and help people in need. It also brought us closer together.

In the fall, Peter prepared to leave for military school while I prepared for medical school. As we kissed goodbye and he held me in his arms, we promised to write each other constant, detailed letters.

"Rachel," he told me, "I will miss you terribly. I treasure each moment that I spend with you. Just remember how much I love you and that at winter break we will be together again." The first semester of school was difficult but exciting. I worked hard and looked forward to winter break. I always worried that Peter's mother would manage to turn him against me, but I told myself that Peter was strong, as were his feelings for me. He would be able to stand up to his mother.

Finally, winter break arrived. How I had been waiting to spend this time with Peter! I went to the hairdresser the day before Peter arrived. I felt excited, yet fearful. I couldn't wait to see him. I wore the pearls my father had given me and when the doorbell finally rang I was ready. My mother disappeared into the kitchen and my father occupied himself with Frida.

I opened the door.

Peter brushed my cheek with a cool kiss, took off his coat and walked to the fireplace to warm his cold hands. Excitedly, I flew to him, covering his face with kisses until I came to his lips. He pressed me close to his chest and our lips met in a long, breathless kiss. "I will never stop loving you," he whispered into my ear. How I had been waiting to hear those words. "I'm so happy that you're home," I whispered back. "Now we can spend every day together. I have so much to tell you, so many stories."

Peter did not answer. Something was wrong. His eyes avoided mine and then he blurted out the news. "I won't be staying home for this winter holiday. I am leaving tomorrow morning for Kłodzko for two weeks." I turned to him in disbelief. "What are you going there for?" Turning his face away from me, he said, "My stepfather's brother lives there and he is always complaining that I never visit. So I have decided to visit him." I could hardly believe what I was hearing. He had never told me about this uncle's existence until this very moment. "Look at me, Peter," I said. "I know that you are hiding something from me." He didn't answer and I burst into tears. I suddenly realized that our relationship was over. The room began to spin. I could hardly catch my breath. I needed fresh air. I needed to calm down. I wiped the tears from my cheeks.

"Fine. I don't need any explanations. It is very clear that you do not love me anymore. I don't want to waste any more of your precious time." Stiffly, he said, "I'm sorry, Rachel. I have to go now but I will stop by to see you before I return to school." I could tell that he wasn't telling me everything, and those unspoken words stood between us like a brick wall. He picked up his coat and walked toward the door. At the door I looked at him and said quietly, "This is goodbye forever, Peter. Do not come by to see me. This door will never be open for you again."

With that, I quickly shut the door and locked it. As I stood with my hand on the doorknob, his footsteps becoming fainter and fainter on the stairs, I knew that an important chapter of my life had just ended. The next morning, I woke to the sun stroking my face. My eyes were swollen and heavy, and a lump had settled in my throat from the night before. I tried to be strong. "Now I am free to devote all of my energy to school and to music." At the breakfast table, my mother could see the change in me. "What happened last night?" The sobs burst from deep inside me. I couldn't speak. My father could not stand to see me suffering. "Don't torture yourself, my little diamond," he told me. "It is not the end of your world. Your dream of love will still come true. Even if Peter doesn't come back, the right person will." Silently, I stood up, put on my coat and went out into the snow for a long walk. Huge snowflakes fell onto my eyelashes, the air was fresh and cold and the sun was so strong it hurt my eyes. I walked the streets for many hours until my face and feet were frozen. When I realized how late it was, I started for home. My family was gentle and understanding with me, and they never mentioned Peter's name again.

Winter vacation passed slowly. We lived near an opera house and my father often got weekend tickets for us to see an opera. Going to the opera became my favourite pastime and sometimes I saw an opera like *Tosca* several times. Occasionally, we went to the Polish Theatre or the Jewish Theatre to see a play directed by Ida Kamińska, the great Jewish theatre star. By the time school started up, I had begun to see my friends again, especially my best girlfriend at the time, Erna Korc. She, too, had survived the war and understood so much about my past and me. We had known each other since Grade 4 and now both of us were studying medicine. From time to time, I ran into Leon. He told me that Peter had been keeping in touch with him and that he wanted to see me again. I always refused.

Chapter 22

In 1955, I was twenty and beginning to settle back into my usual routine. My heart still ached for Peter, but I hid my feelings. By this time our house was full of children. Uncle Shiko and Aunt Regina had another little boy, Hanoch, born in 1954 and named for Regina's father. Frida was ten and Eli, six. I adored all the children, but felt more like their caretaker than sister and cousin. I knew every single detail of their lives from the moment they were born, but they knew very little about my past and my childhood, each having been born after the war. No one ever asked me and I did not volunteer. I had no privacy, but I still felt isolated, keeping my memories and past bottled up inside me.

As always, change enters our lives at the moment we least expect it. And so it was for me that year.

That September, a week before Rosh Hashanah, I had a visit from an old friend, Baruch Kochman, whom we called Bucio. Bucio had been Luci's long-time boyfriend and my parents knew Bucio's family so well that he called my parents "uncle" and "aunt." I had not seen him in over two years, since his break-up with Luci. When he came into the living room, settling himself comfortably into the large, brown leather chair, he seemed pleased to find that nothing had changed. He asked me about my studies, friends and Peter. It was good to see an old friend and to have someone care to ask. As I spoke, my eyes filled with tears. But when I asked about his life he seemed distracted. Turning his head to the clock, he suddenly leapt up. "I have to run, Rachel, I'm sorry. I have a friend, Adam, arriving from Warsaw and I have to pick him up at the train station. I am afraid that I will be late." When he saw my disappointment, he asked, "Why don't you walk with me and we can continue our conversation?" I quickly grabbed my purse, fixed my hair and we were off.

The main station was within walking distance of my house and we moved quickly through the busy street. People rushed by in all directions and the streetcars were full and overflowing. We pushed our way through traffic and crossed the street to the train station. When we arrived, they were already announcing that the train from Warsaw was arriving on time.

Bucio was excited, walking back and forth, looking for his friend. It took a long time until all the passengers left the train. No Adam. Bucio was confused – perhaps he had misunderstood and Adam was meant to arrive the next day. Disappointed, he put his arm around me and told me he would take me home.

As we walked, I wondered why Bucio was really in town. It all seemed so strange. When we reached the entrance to our building, he stopped. "Rachel, can I ask you a favour?" "Of course," I said, curious now. "I must go home now, but I will be back tomorrow. I hope that you don't mind, but I gave Adam your address and told him that in case we missed each other at the station, he could meet me at your house." He kissed me lightly on the cheek and smiled. "Give my regards to your parents."

"Wait!" I called out after him. "Don't leave yet." Now I was really curious. He was acting very strangely. "Please stay for the evening. There is a dance tonight at the Jewish Students' Club and I need a date. Please say that you will come with me." He looked into my eyes. I smiled. I knew he would not refuse.

My mother was happy to see Bucio and, as always, was ready for company with dinner. She studied my face, looking for hints. I had suddenly come to life. I had not been this happy in a long while. I could tell she was hoping something was developing here. "Bucio's staying and taking me to the dance tonight," I told her.

Throughout dinner my father and Bucio talked. Frida, as always, tried to bring all eyes to her corner, arguing with mother about finishing all the food on her plate. I drifted in and out of the conversation, contemplating the strange turn of events. I was confused by Bucio's reluctance to talk about himself earlier. Why didn't he answer any of my questions? I sensed that he was hiding something and hoped that I would be able to figure it all out by the end of the evening. It had been a long time since I felt this excited.

Finally, when dessert and tea were served, I excused myself. Rushing to my bedroom, I took my favourite blue dress out of the closet. I had not worn it since Peter and I had broken up. With my royal blue chamois-leather high heels and pearl necklace, I began to feel very festive. I checked my hair in the mirror and sprayed on my favourite fragrance, lily of the valley. I was ready to go.

On the street, Bucio waved down a taxi. We settled into the car and Bucio explained to the driver that we were going to the Jewish Congress Building on Włodkowica Street. The Jewish Congress in Wrocław had been formed after the war to help Holocaust survivors pick up the tattered pieces of their lives. The building was a very important place for the Jews of the city. It housed many different activities: a space for adult technical courses sponsored by the Organization for Rehabilitation through Training, or ORT (where Uncle Shiko learned his trade of watch repair and Aunt Regina learned to sew men's shirts and pyjamas, and women's lingerie); a children's nursery; a space for groups and volunteer organizations to meet; and a practice space for the mandolin group, Orfeusz. In the courtyard there was a student hostel and, most importantly, an Orthodox synagogue where Jewish families could gather and pray. During the High Holidays, at Rosh Hashanah and Yom Kippur, my family attended this synagogue. On Yom Kippur, we lit candles for our dear ones who perished in the war. I looked forward to the times when I could meet my friends outside in the courtyard. It was as though I was a young girl back in Turka.

Though it had been ten years since the war ended, this area had still not taken on a new face. Most of the buildings had been completely destroyed during the war and only a few partially destroyed buildings stood stoically, here and there. Many families, my friend Erna's included, had chosen to settle here, supporting their ceilings with iron beams and making the best of a battered area in order to establish a new home.

When we reached the tall, grey, bullet-ridden stone building, we could hear that the party had already begun. Swing music wafted through the street and high-spirited voices greeted us as we rushed up the stairs to the entrance, caught our breath and looked around for familiar faces. The large rectangular room had a stage at one end with an old-fashioned, time-worn piano and a dark red-velvet curtain as a backdrop. The walls were decorated with pictures of important officials, in the centre of which Stalin, Lenin and Marx smiled down on us. Although it was very crowded with people standing around happily and sitting in little groups talking excitedly, Bucio found two chairs for us against the wall near the window.

As we sat down, the band started to play the song "Bésame Mucho," and Bucio asked me to dance. I reached for his hand, a big smile on my face, and we joined the dancers on the floor. I loved to dance and enjoyed the compliments I always got. Because of the Gypsies of my childhood, I melted each time I heard the sentimental strains of their music, especially the violin, and remembered their vivacious and stirring dances. When the rumba ended, Bucio led me back to my chair and I glanced around the room. I was watching the long counter where volunteers had spread out open-faced sandwiches, portions of gefilte fish, hot tea and cold bottled lemonade. It was then that I noticed my cousin, Luci, and her current boyfriend, Abraham.

Abraham looked quite nervous, fidgeting with a cigarette, lighting it as he stood in conversation with his friends. Luci had seen me enter the room with Bucio and she looked surprised and shocked, especially since I had told her I would not be coming to the dance at all. There she stood next to Abraham, pretending not to have seen me, laughing a little too loudly, trying to call attention to herself and impress their friends.

The band began to play a waltz and I asked Bucio to dance with me again. As we moved across the floor, I noticed some of my friends whispering and looking at us, but I didn't care if there were rumours. We looked good together. I danced all evening, not missing a single tune, either with Bucio or occasionally with other friends. All evening, Bucio avoided Luci. He was nervous, but I was having too good a time to take him seriously. At eleven o'clock, he turned to me and said, "Rachel, let me take you home now. I have to catch the midnight bus tonight to Legnica." "Stay overnight at our place," I begged, "I am having such a good time. Don't spoil it. Let's stay to the..." Bucio didn't wait for me to finish. There was something on his mind. "Rachel," he stumbled, "I would love to stay, but I can't." Finally, he had to say it. "I don't know how to tell you this. I'm a married man." I couldn't believe my ears. "Are you serious?" "Yes," he said shyly. "Not only am I married, but we're expecting a child. I don't know why I did not tell you sooner."

Why had he kept this marriage a secret? Was he embarrassed because he had not invited me to the wedding? Why hadn't he told Luci? I wanted to ask him all of these questions, but somehow couldn't. "I understand, Bucio. Go. I will stay until the end and get a ride home with Luci." After Bucio left, I joined Luci and her crowd. We spent the rest of the evening chatting and dancing and laughing, but she did not ask me about Bucio or tell me how she felt seeing him again. And I did not tell her his secret.

When the party broke at three o'clock in the morning, I was exhausted and settled quite happily into the back seat of Abraham's car.

I had called my mother earlier and told her that I would be sleeping at Luci's. I was glad. There were no children there and on Sunday morning I would be able to sleep in without any disturbances. As I lay in the dark, falling asleep, the events of the entire incredible day went through my mind. For the first time in a long time, I felt optimistic about the future. Someone would come along who would appreciate me just as I am and no one would be able to take him away from me. I lulled myself to sleep with the strong feeling that there were changes coming into my life. I had completely forgotten about Bucio's friend, Adam, who would be arriving at my house in the morning.

Chapter 23

It has become a story that Adam has retold to our children and friends over the years. A simple adventure, our meeting has become a tale about fate and how random meetings become lives shared forever. "It was a beautiful Sunday morning," he always begins. "The air was alive with warmth and sunshine. Although it was still early September, the golden shades of autumn were already softly lending their charm to nature."

The train had not been crowded and he had slept through the night on the upper compartment where suitcases were usually stacked. Though this was not as comfortable as a bed, he was able to settle down for the long twelve-hour trip and awoke to the announcement of the train's arrival. He was excited and ready for an interesting day in a new city.

When Adam reached the exit gate of the station, he looked around for his friend Bucio. Not seeing him right away, he decided to wait a little. He bought a newspaper, *Trybuna Ludu*, to pass the time, but felt agitated that Bucio might have forgotten to come. He quickly became impatient and then suddenly remembered the address near the train station that Bucio had given him in case he wasn't able to make it on time. That, Adam was sure, was where Bucio would be. After asking directions, he walked out into the morning.

"At six o'clock in the morning, the streets were still empty and quiet," he goes on to tell. "I was surprised at the state of the streets in this area, where nothing had been repaired since the war. There wasn't even a sidewalk. I walked in the middle of the road, stepping over the rubble, and wondered if I could possibly be in the right place. Stopping a passerby, I asked again about the address and about twenty minutes later I saw, in the distance, the six-apartment-building complex I had been told to expect. "Finally!" I thought. As I came closer, I could see the many bullet holes in the brick walls of the buildings. Again, I looked at the instructions. Yes, this was it: Dworcowa Street No. 4, Apartment 4.

At the top of the stairs, Adam folded his beige trench coat over his left arm, held his newspaper in his right hand and, glancing at his watch, he noticed uneasily that it was only seven a.m. He rang the doorbell twice and waited. When my mother opened the door, she was smiling. She knew Adam would be coming and she was prepared.

"I am Adam Shtibel," he said, "and I apologize for disturbing you so early in the morning." "Please come in," my mother said, motioning toward the living room. "Bucio was here yesterday and we have been expecting you. I'm sure he will be here soon." Relaxed now that he had found the right place, Adam was glad there seemed to be nice people living here. He reached out for my mother's hand and kissed it, as was a customary sign of respect to a lady in Poland.

At this point in the story, my mother always added that she was very impressed with this gentlemanly gesture. "None of Rachel's friends were so courteous," she would muse. He had captured her heart, right then and there. She showed him into Shiko's small living room, which was off to the side of the long hallway and separate from the other rooms. "My name is Sara Milbauer. Please make yourself at home and have a seat." She went off to the kitchen where Aunt Regina was waiting for her, curious about the stranger in the living room. They stood together, wondering what to do next. Where was Bucio? And why had Rachel not returned home yet?

Adam looked around the room, taking in the surroundings. The yellow canary chirped noisily in his cage on the wide windowsill. He wondered to himself, Who are these people? And where was Bucio? Even though he felt uncomfortable, he liked the cozy, warm atmosphere. Since childhood, when he had lost his entire family in the war, he had dreamed of being part of a happy family again. Oh, how lucky Bucio is, Adam thought in frustration, if this is his girlfriend's family. My mother returned to the stranger in the living room with freshly percolated coffee and hot cinnamon buns. She was very taken with him.

It was late morning when Bubbie Yetta woke me. "Rachel baby, get up. Remember that friend of Bucio's from Warsaw? He's at your house, waiting." I jumped up, suddenly remembering. Half asleep, I threw on my clothes and rushed out the door, annoyed by the imposition.

Aunt Regina opened the door and in a whisper began to tell me about our guest. I told her I didn't care about him and that I was going to tell him to wait for Bucio if he wanted to, but that I was going back to bed. My mother joined us and she and Aunt Regina pressed me to stay and keep Adam company until Bucio came, telling me that it was not polite to ignore him. Grudgingly, I realized that even though I was very tired and looked a mess, I had no choice. "Is he good-looking, at least?" I asked, sarcastically. "See for yourself," they whispered in unison.

I knocked quietly on the living room door, so as not to startle him, and entered. Our eyes met. "I'm Rachel," I said, surprised at how handsome he was, and reached out to shake his hand.

"I'm Adam," he said, looking up over his open newspaper and stretching out his hand. Strange, I thought, how I feel that I want to get to know him better. Suddenly, I wasn't tired anymore. He stood up, his dark brown, almond-shaped eyes gazing at me out of a heart-shaped face. He had curly, thick black hair, combed up from his large forehead. And he had beautiful full lips. I looked at the shape of his hands and fingers and felt the urge to touch them and be touched by them. His voice rang in my ears and his warmth embraced me. I could not believe my reaction to this stranger in my living room.

My mother prepared a royal breakfast for us and I offered to show Adam the city. It was obvious to both of us now that Bucio would not be coming. I wanted to show him everything, especially the exhibition grounds where we could go on rides. I knew that he could only stay until the last train left the city that night and I wanted to spend as much time with him as possible. We grabbed our coats and, holding hands, walked to the nearby park. We stopped at the bridge and watched the golden fish in the stream. Adam looked like a tourist dressed in his dark brown suit and tie, his trench coat over his arm and his camera around his neck. He took pictures of me and asked a passing man to take pictures of both of us together. How quickly we seemed to have become a couple. My head was spinning.

"Oh, Adam, this is going to be a great day!" I told him excitedly. We walked for a long time in the park and I told him about Bucio's visit the day before. He told me about his life in Warsaw and about his struggle to hang on to his apartment. Even though it was only a one-bedroom apartment, it was considered too large for a single occupant by the Communist authorities in charge of housing who assigned living spaces by size. As I listened to him, I could sense that Adam was as taken with me as I was with him. How very different he was from Peter. He was strong and seemed so mature. I admired his ability to make serious decisions on his own and carry out his responsibilities with no guidance or help. I was fascinated by him.

Walking through the park, I felt very flattered that he felt comfortable enough with me to tell me about his ex-fiancée, Dora. She had recently broken up with him and cancelled their wedding. He told me that I looked very much like her, but that my personality and character were very different from hers. He hadn't felt this good for a long time, he said. He confided that for the first time since their break-up, he was able to forget about Dora and feel happy. But he was afraid too, he said, that something would happen and the chance at the happiness he might be discovering with me would be taken away. My heart beat wildly and I could hardly breathe as he spoke. I had just met this man and he was already afraid of losing me.

As Adam talked about himself, we walked slowly to the streetcar that would take us to the exhibition grounds on the outskirts of the city. That part of the city was new and showed no signs of war and destruction. Adam was very impressed with the grounds and especially admired the public hall, the Hala Ludowa, that was in the centre. The focal point of the grounds, the hall was a huge round building that had the capacity to accommodate thousands of people and was the pride of Wrocław. It was equipped with a huge rotating stage that took up most of the interior; many famous performers appeared there. As I looked around, I thought back to the concert long ago when I played the czardas and Rita had performed her Gypsy dance on that very stage.

Adam and I strolled around. He took my hand, keeping me close to him. We had so much to tell each other. I forgot all about the rides and attractions around us, passing by them without notice. When we came to a bench, Adam spread his coat on the seat and asked me to sit down for a while. Holding my hands, he pulled me closer to him as he spoke. Usually when I listened to someone speak for a long time, I would eventually find my mind wandering off into my own little daydreams. But with Adam I was attached to each and every word that he spoke.

We had become so engrossed in each other in that single day that I had forgotten that Adam did not live in Wrocław. Now it occurred to me that he would have to leave soon. As if he could read my mind, he put his head close to mine and began to speak quietly. "Rachel, there is no one else in my life. I cannot tell you everything about my life right now, but I will tell you everything in time. I have only one female friend, Wioletta. She lives with her grandmother but is officially registered with the authorities as living with me. There is nothing between us, but the only way I can keep my apartment is if the government thinks more than one person lives there. I want to hold on to this apartment for the day when, hopefully, I will be married and will need a large space for my family. Families that sign up for an apartment now are on waiting lists that last for years."

As I listened to his story, I began to feel uneasy. I was strangely hurt when he mentioned the girl. How could I trust this complete stranger? Maybe they were living together. I should have known that this feeling was too good to be true. I would not build my hopes up and be hurt again. There was no point in listening any further and risking more pain.

"It's getting late... and dark," Adam said, again reading my mind. "Let me take you home. I have to catch the ten o'clock train back. This way I'll travel all night and be able to go straight to work from the station in the morning." He looked at me closely and asked in a soft voice, "Rachel, will you write me?" I did not answer and we headed back to the streetcar. On the hour-long ride home I was afraid to be happy. I felt a great emptiness inside me and was already worried about how much I knew I would miss him when he left.

"He must have been a very interesting person," my mother probed, "for you to have spent a whole day with him, especially since you were so tired this morning." Adam joined us for dinner and I sat quietly as my father and Uncle Shiko talked with him about his family and about work. He told them how his entire family had perished in the war and that he had been on his own since the age of eleven. He hid in forests and villages, and after the war he was taken to live in an orphanage in Warsaw. Later, when he was living at a student hostel in Warsaw, he told his story to the representatives of the Central Jewish Historical Commission in Warsaw and they recorded it and placed it in their archives. He told us about his only living relative, Gedaliusz, a distant cousin who had survived the war in the Soviet Union and was now living with his family in Legnica. He visited them often and it was there he met Bucio.

As I listened to him speak so openly and honestly, I looked around the table and could see that my family was as moved by Adam as I was. This was a boy who had been through a great deal and we could all relate to that. I felt my heart lightening. My mind was made up. I would fight for Adam. I suddenly felt very grownup.

As if sensing the mood of everyone at the table, Adam suddenly changed the topic of conversation. He told us about all he had accomplished in the few years since the war ended. He had joined the Polish air force and had become a pilot flying Yak-9 fighter planes. When he completed that course, he was among only ten other pilots chosen for training on MIG-3 fighter jets. Unfortunately, a few weeks before the course was to begin, he was suddenly removed from his military base and told not to contact his colleagues again. The officials, he later found out, had checked on his past and discovered that he had belonged to the Zionist youth organization Hashomer Hatzair after the war. He had not told them about this and they took that to mean that he was somehow connected to Israel. For the authorities, this was enough proof that he posed a great threat to the security of the Polish air force.

Adam was devastated by his dismissal, but immediately applied to a civilian airline company for work. He was bluntly told that he would never find work as a pilot with a civilian airline because he had been expelled from the air force. He was now working as a technician in a government factory, building small airplanes. He had been taking special evening courses at the Technical Engineering School in Warsaw and had recently accepted an offer to work as an electronic parts inspector for the National Polish Telecommunications Company. "I make a good living," he told us, "but I am very lonely."

Chapter 24

Our wedding date was set for June 24, 1956. This was to be the first celebration for my family in a very long time and our house was alive with excitement and activity. The simple invitations were sent out a month before the wedding and my father booked musicians, including a violinist. Uncle Shiko volunteered to be the photographer. We would have the wedding at home, opening up the apartment so that Shiko's and our sections were joined. The furniture would be rearranged to accommodate tables covered with white tablecloths along the walls. The head table was to be arranged in the middle of the room where my grand piano stood with the band. We hired two women from our synagogue to prepare the meal. For weeks before the wedding, they were busy baking breads and cakes and cooking traditional Jewish foods. The menu at the wedding would begin with challah and gefilte fish, go on to chicken soup with Bubbie Yetta's thin egg noodles, roast beef, roast duck, cabbage rolls, boiled potatoes with fresh dill and *tzimmes*, a sweet carrot pudding. For dessert there would be non-dairy ice cream and my mother's "best in the world" apple strudel.

Two weeks before the wedding, I was at home studying when a young lady knocked at the door. She told me her name was Wioletta and that she was from Warsaw. I recalled that Adam had mentioned her on his first visit. When I saw her at the door, I immediately feared something had happened to Adam. She assured me that he was fine and that she had come because she needed to speak to me personally. "You know," she blurted out, "that I live with Adam and I came to tell you that I am pregnant." I nearly fainted. Trying to keep my composure, I slowly stood up and said, "All right, I will not stand in your way – my wedding is in two weeks, but I will cancel it and even wish you both good luck." She seemed surprised and a bit thrown off by my answer. "I don't want to marry Adam!" she shrieked, "I want you to give me money for an abortion." I looked at her in amazement. "Don't you think you should discuss this with Adam, not me?" "Adam does not want to marry me. He loves you," she continued, matter-of-factly. "He doesn't even know that I am here and asking for your help." Something was wrong with this wild story. I felt suddenly numb. After thinking for a moment, I told her to leave her phone number with me and that I would reach her by the end of the day.

When she finally left, the tears began to flow. I told my mother and Regina about Wioletta and her unbelievable story. They were speechless. Seeing their shock broke something inside me. I had been afraid that something would go wrong – and it had. When my father and Shiko returned from work we all discussed the situation. My father was as strong as always and told me, "I still believe that Adam is a good man and that he will be a wonderful husband to you. You must talk to him and hear his side of the story. We'll give her the money if that's what she wants, but you must give Adam a chance."

I called Wioletta and asked her how much she wanted. When I heard the exorbitant amount I told her I would have to get back to her in a few days. Immediately, I purchased an airplane ticket to Warsaw. I cried throughout the entire flight and was not sure I would be able to find the strength to face Adam.

When I arrived, Adam was his usual warm and loving self, even though I had arrived unexpectedly. Sitting in his tiny kitchen, I told him about Wioletta's visit. He swore to me that there had been no other woman in his life since he and I had met. He was furious with

Wioletta for having the gall to lie to me about him and her pregnancy. "She must have become pregnant with someone who would not help her and she has no money of her own to resolve the situation herself." I could see that he was thinking about something. "Finally, things are beginning to become clear," he said. "You know that she has a key to my apartment because she is officially registered under my address. Last week, I came home to find my apartment emptied – everything, including my clothes. I thought I had been robbed. I obviously was – by Wioletta – who stole my belongings to sell." He was pacing up and down, screaming with rage. "She probably read all of your letters! She probably isn't even pregnant! How dare she threaten our happiness? She is a thief and a liar!"

Adam sat down next to me and reached for my hand. He was beside himself. "Please, please, Rachel, you have to believe me. I love you and it is only with you that I want to share my life and future." He suddenly became very stern. "You cannot, you must not, give her a penny!" I looked into his warm, gentle eyes and knew he was telling me the truth. I did trust him.

When I returned home, I told my father what Adam had told me and he insisted that we give Wioletta the money she asked for. "You don't want her to be a stain on your wedding day. We must have her out of our lives forever." After Wioletta received the money from my father, we never heard from her again.

⁓

As is customary in a Jewish Orthodox wedding, Adam and I fasted the day before our wedding and were not permitted to see each other for the twenty-four hours prior to the ceremony. Adam stayed at my parents' house and I went to stay with my mother's cousins, Isaac and Ewa Zweig. The morning of the wedding, June 24, 1956, I came home to find the entire apartment transformed.

Regina and Shiko's small living room had been turned into a bride's room. In the corner there was an armchair covered with a white sheet. It was surrounded by an ocean of flowers and behind it the walls were decorated with mirrors. This is where I was to sit and greet all the women who came in. I felt like a princess. Breathlessly, I awaited the evening.

Adam was a very handsome groom in his navy blue suit and white bow tie. His black wavy hair shone and his wonderful smile brightened his whole face. In his warm, dark eyes I could read his happiness and undying love for me. It only added to my joy that my parents also loved Adam and already considered him a son. Finally, Adam's prayers would be answered. He would once again be part of a warm and loving family.

My princess-style wedding dress was a soft, off-white gown with a long lace veil. I carried a bouquet of fresh white roses that matched the wreath I wore in my hair. As I walked on the white sheet covering the floor, toward my future, the children walked in front of me, sprinkling white rose petals in my path. The house, festive and full of flowers, seemed a beautiful rose garden to me and a fitting symbol of this glorious day full of laughter and tears of happiness.

Today, I can still see before me the eighty-two-year-old rabbi who performed the ceremony. When we were ready to break our fast, Adam and I were served sponge cake and freshly-brewed coffee. I don't remember eating anything else that night, but I can see, as clearly as if it were yesterday, my bubbie Yetta dancing toward the centre of the head table where we sat with a two-metre-long braided challah. There were a hundred guests, including Jozef and Rozalia Beck, and our unwitting matchmaker, Bucio, who was our guest of honour and whom we shall bless all of our lives.

The only cloud on my happy day was Luci's absence. The person with whom I had spent my entire childhood – the happy times and the terrible times – and the one who truly knew what this day meant for me and for my family, had not found it important enough to attend. She told me later that she had not been able to come because she had made other plans with her boyfriend, Abraham.

The celebration lasted into the early hours of the morning. When each guest left, they were given a beautifully-wrapped white napkin full of wedding sweets to take home. For the next few days, family and friends continued to come by to wish us well. My father was right. Adam turned out not only to be the best husband for me but also my best friend.

Chapter 25

During our month-long honeymoon in Międzyzdroje on the Baltic Sea, Adam and I discovered that we both loved nature, especially the countryside, because it reminded both of us of our early childhood. Both of us were children of the Holocaust and we talked a great deal about the war and our losses. By the end of our first week together there was nothing we hadn't told each other.

After a long debate, Adam and I decided that we would give up his apartment in Warsaw and that we would live with my parents. Even though Adam had a great job in Warsaw, we both felt that it was important for us to be together while I finished my fourth year of medical studies. This was not an easy choice. Adam would have a hard time finding work in Wrocław – he was not only a Jew, he was also new to the city and did not belong to the Communist Party. These factors would make it extremely difficult for him find work in his field, particularly in any government-owned company.

In the summer of 1956, Jews in high positions were being removed from their jobs and the Polish government was opening the borders for Jews in the hope of getting rid of them. Around this time, I came home from lectures one day to find my family huddled together with grave expressions on their faces. We had received a letter from the government stating that all Jewish first names must be changed immediately to Polish names. Furthermore, all family names were to be changed to Polish spelling. Foreign spellings would not be allowed.

For days, my father and Shiko discussed what to do. They knew very well that if we resisted we would be in danger. They finally agreed that we would change the spelling of our family name from Muhlbauer to Milbauer. For the sake of safety and survival, we were also forced to change our Jewish first names to Polish names. The humiliation and disgust we felt at changing our names makes it impossible for me to even write those names here. Was it not over? Would it begin again? Our names were all we had left.

Adam found profitable work buying and selling a new product – the "Moto-Rower." This was a bicycle with a small engine attached. Adam would travel to Katowice, a city near Bytom in Upper Silesia. Once every two years, the coal miners received a coupon to purchase this motorized bicycle. After buying the coupons from the miners, Adam would present them at the appropriate store and receive the bicycles with no questions asked. Then he would ship them to Wrocław. In Wrocław, he was able to sell the bicycles for higher prices to Jewish people who could not get the coupons.

My father and Shiko now made efforts to secure permission for all of us to immigrate to Israel. It was the only place we believed we could live as Jews and be safe. This was not the first time we had applied to leave. We had already submitted three applications over the past few years, but my father applied again, this time adding Adam's name to the application. Finally, in late 1956, we received news that our application to leave Poland for Israel had been approved. My father, however, insisted that Adam and I stay in Poland so that I could complete my medical degree. I would not hear of it. There had not been a moment when we had been separated of our own free will and I was not going to allow it.

Before we left for Israel, my father went back to Turka. "One last time, I want to see my birthplace and visit the people who helped us." He decided he would take Frida, who was eleven years old, and Eli, who was seven, to show them where we had lived. I was very upset that my father was not taking me with him on this journey. I also wanted to see my home for the last time, to be again in the surroundings I treasured. I never really knew why he did not take me, whether it was because he thought it would bring back painful memories of the past or because he did not want me to look back, only forward. Turka was then a part of the USSR, not Poland, and perhaps he felt more secure travelling with small children. That way he could say he was on vacation rather than spark the suspicion of the Soviet authorities at the border that he was on some other mission. He purchased the tickets, arranged for passports and they left for Kołomyja.

When they returned, my father brought back memories of the past. He told us that the village of Turka had not been damaged by the war and was just as we had left it. The orchard was as beautiful as it had always been. He had knocked on the door of our old house and told the peasant woman that this had been his family's house before the war and that he had planted the apple trees. He asked her if he could pick a few apples so he could taste, one last time, the fruits of his past labours. She agreed and, tearfully, he picked his apples.

He had also gone to visit Vasil and Maria Olehrecky, the couple hired to help on my grandparents' farm who had become our saviours during the war. My father found Vasil still living on his farm, but he and Maria had divorced and both had new spouses. My father gave him money and gifts and thanked him again for all he had done for us. Like brothers, they hugged and cried and said their goodbyes. My father went to see Maria and also gave her gifts and money. He told them both that we were immigrating to Israel and that we would never see them again. They both asked that my father not write to them from Israel, as the political situation in the USSR at this time made them afraid they would be accused of having "contacts" with Israel. These visits were very emotional and painful for all of them and brought back the memories of the life we had lived and tragically lost. Finally, my father went to visit the parents of my childhood friend,

Mecio. He told them I was a medical student. Mecio, they told him, was studying engineering.

My father told us how the Jews in the Soviet Union were scrambling to get out of the country. While he was staying with a Jewish family in Kołomyja, many of their friends had come to speak to him. They pleaded with him to help them get out of the USSR. He showed us the long list of Jewish families he had promised to sponsor and help immigrate to Poland as a step toward going to Israel. We looked at him in surprise, but he was adamant. "I need to give back, to do for others in need what those like Vasil and Jozef did for us when we were in grave danger and desperate. I cannot turn my back. It is a mitzvah."

There was nothing to say. The next day we all set to work. We divided the list and Shiko, Regina, Adam, my mother and father and I began to arrange official papers for "the relatives" whom we would be sponsoring so we could all be "reunited in Poland."

~

In the beginning, I had mixed feelings about leaving Poland. I had been raised in Poland, my roots were there, and I loved the country whose culture, language, history and tradition were in my blood. The first few times my father spoke about applying for permission to go to Israel, I was angry. "My place is in Poland," I told him. "I'm staying right here." Living in a Communist country, I had never listened to the radio news beyond the Iron Curtain and could not compare my life in Poland to anywhere else. I had no idea what Israel was like. I knew only that it was very hot. I remembered how ecstatic my family had been when Israel became an independent state in 1948, but for me, that new homeland was very remote.

But as time passed and the situation for Jews in Poland worsened, I began to look forward to the world beyond. Adam and I would be able to start a new life in Israel where we would be able to raise a Jewish family without fear. It felt like a dream to be free and equal to all other citizens. Again I could use my own Hebrew name. I longed for the time I would not have to be afraid to be Jewish.

Two weeks before we were to leave for Israel, our house gradually began to fill with immigrants from the USSR who had nowhere else to go. Eventually, there were so many people living in our apartment that it began to remind me of the cargo train, full of cigarette smoke, mattresses and loud, hopeful voices that had brought us to Poland from Kołomyja after the war. My mother was cooking all the time, as if for an army, but was happy to contribute. We were going to help these people be free. Finally, the doors to the world would open, not only for us, but for them as well.

Nostalgia and sadness overcame me on our last day in Poland. We were leaving the soil where our ancestors had lived and where so many of us had tragically perished. We knew we would never return. As usual, my father tried to cheer us up and told us, "This is our last evening in Wrocław and we are going to the opera. I have tickets for *Tosca* and even though we have seen this opera many times before, I want this night to be a night to remember." And so it was.

Part Four: Israel

Chapter 26

We arrived in Israel on February 28, 1957. We soon discovered that life here would be very different from life in Europe. The climate was hot and humid, and Hebrew was a very difficult language to master. My father had originally wanted to settle on a farm, but now that he was older, he knew it would be too great an effort for him. He and Uncle Shiko bought a small grocery store in Jaffa, on the outskirts of Tel Aviv, and we found a place to live together close to the store.

Our house was the third in from the sea on a small street, Ha-Kovshim. It took us a while to get used to the smells and sounds of the sea at our doorstep. Adam and I took a five-month course to learn Hebrew. When we finished, Adam applied for a job in the aircraft industry, Bedek. He was accepted as an airplane parts inspector and was very happy there.

Meanwhile, my father and I went to Jerusalem to inquire about whether I would be accepted to the faculty of medicine. The dean informed us that there would be no problem finding medical courses for me. However, the program in Poland was very different from the one in Israel and, as a result, I would have to go back to second year. This meant that I would essentially lose two years of study. Also, instead of the five-year course I was on in Poland, medical studies in Israel lasted seven years and were only offered in Jerusalem. To this day,

I am not sure I made the right decision, but I refused the acceptance. The dean offered to accept me to either pharmacy or bacteriology, also in the second year, but at least these degrees only took four years. Out of frustration, I agreed to do a course in pharmacy. This meant that I had to stay in Jerusalem to study. Meanwhile, Adam lived with my family in Jaffa so he could continue at his job.

It was during that first year in Israel, back at school, that I became pregnant. It was a very difficult pregnancy. I sometimes fainted, developed toxemia and was very swollen. On October 29, 1958, I delivered a beautiful baby girl, whom we named Batia after Adam's mother, who had perished in the Holocaust. In English, we call her Barbara. The baby looked like Adam, with dark curly hair, a fair complexion and dark brown eyes.

After Barbara was born I became deeply depressed. I was sure I was dying of an incurable disease that my family was keeping secret from me. I had no interest in the baby and was afraid to be alone. I had returned to Jaffa to be with Adam, the baby and my family. When Adam was away at work, my mother took care of the baby and me. Often I fainted during the day. Many times, my mother had to call the doctor because I became hysterical, crying that I was dying and that no one was paying any attention to me. On several occasions when I was at home alone with my sleeping baby, I entertained the thought of jumping out the window. I wanted to end my miserable life and stop being a burden to everyone. But I couldn't. Standing in front of the open window, the thought of leaving my baby all alone was too much for me and I quickly closed the window, backed as far away from it as I could, and ran to my baby. I never told anyone about these incidents, but continued to struggle with my health for the entire year that followed.

When Adam came home from work, I would beg him, "Please, tell me what's wrong with me. Am I going to die?" He would hold me close, kiss my forehead and quietly tell me, "I assure you, you are not dying. You will be just fine. The doctor says this is just a bad time for you and that it will pass." I would fall asleep in his arms, finally at peace. He was the only person in the world I trusted.

When I was ready to resume my studies, I applied to the Tel Aviv University so I could be closer to home. They did not have a faculty of pharmacy or medicine, so I entered the third year of microbiology. Soon Adam and I moved into our own little apartment in Lod, a city near the airport, so Adam could be close to his work. My mother was a great help to us with the baby, who stayed with my parents while I studied. This was not easy for my mother for she had become a sick woman. Before we left Poland, Dr. Nieder had warned her never to stop taking the insulin injections. He told her that there would soon be pills on the market, but for her it would be very dangerous and life-threatening to stop the injections.

It was extremely difficult for me to be separated from my baby while I studied. On one of my visits from the university, I found my daughter playing with her friends. "Look," she said, pointing, as she saw me coming toward her, "I do have a mommy." Hearing her say this broke my heart and made me even more determined to work hard and finish quickly so that I could have my baby home with me.

Finally, in June 1964, when Barbara was five years old, I graduated from Tel Aviv University with a master's degree in microbiology. My proud parents, my loving husband, Adam, and my little daughter, Barbara, were all there at my graduation with huge bouquets of red roses. It was an emotional moment for all of us. My father placed a beautiful gold necklace around my neck and gold-and-pearl earrings in my hand. I knew what this moment meant to him and I will always treasure his gifts. Adam surprised me with the newest transistor radio from Japan, a Hitachi that I had been dreaming about. I had a surprise of my own for them, too. I was pregnant with my second baby.

After graduation, I applied to work at the Kaplan Hospital in the city of Rehovot. I was offered a position in the bacteriology department as a senior scientist working on identifying complicated bacterial organisms, studying their susceptibility to antibacterial drugs, and writing reports for the doctors. Suddenly, life was good again. I was working. We could afford a babysitter for our daughter, who had come back to live with us. I was pregnant again and it was going smoothly. My parents, whenever they visited us, were proud of our growing little family and how well we were managing.

I was also receiving a very good salary and our financial situation had improved a great deal. I decided I would begin to think about my piano. When I had been a student, with only Adam's salary to support us, our financial situation had left us no choice but to sell my precious piano. This had been incredibly painful for me. Adam had tried to comfort me. "One day, when you finish your studies and we can afford it, you will have a piano again. I promise." My second daughter was born on December 2, 1964, at Kaplan Hospital, where I worked. We named her after Bubbie Yetta, who had passed away a few years earlier. We had suffered greatly over the loss of my grandmother, but now the joy of a new life was coming into our lives. In English, we call her Iris. While I was in the hospital, Adam had the apartment painted, prepared the baby's room and hung pretty curtains. Our little home was beautiful. It was decided that my mother would stay with me for a week when I came home from the hospital.

My mother busied herself happily by cooking, baking and preparing everything so that it would be easier for me with the new baby. After the week was up, she decided to go home to see how my father and sister were managing on their own. Her plan was to prepare some food for them that would last a few days and then come back to be with me.

But my mother had been neglecting her health. Disregarding Dr. Nieder's advice, she had switched from injections to diabetic pills. She felt that her body needed a break from the injections, but she soon found herself facing serious complications. Her blood sugar levels were out of control and her kidneys were so damaged that she needed surgery. At that time in Israel, when one needed surgery, family members were obligated to donate the blood that the patient needed.

Adam and my father wanted to give blood to the blood bank for her, but their blood types did not match. My mother's blood type, AB, was rare, and my father had type B and Adam, type O. They had to find her blood type somewhere else. Another serious complication was that my mother was going blind. Diabetes had affected her eyes and Adam took her to many specialists, but at that time, no treatments were available. The damage she had caused to her body by stopping her insulin injections would prove fatal.

On the last day of her visit, my mother touched the baby's face and said, "I can hardly see today, everything is blurry, but I can feel her features and she will be very beautiful." As we hugged and kissed goodbye, we cried together. I did not know it would be the last time I saw my mother. The next day she suffered a heart attack and died in the hospital. She was fifty-seven years old. Aunt Mina and her family were already living in Canada at that time, but my father and Adam were with her at the end.

Chapter 27

The loss of my mother was very difficult for me. I felt I could not go on without her. Every time I looked out the window I thought I saw her coming from the distance. I was afraid to be alone in the house. I prepared bottles for the baby and took the stroller out in the morning and only came home when I knew Adam would be home from work. I cried constantly and was in a very bad emotional state. My baby never saw a smile on my face. I was surprised that Iris even knew how to smile and that she was a happy child.

My father was very lonely. He missed my mother but did not want to live with us. He wanted to be in the lovely home in Holon that he and my mother had moved to just a few months before her death. So we decided to move closer to my father, even though it meant that Adam and I would have to travel further to work. Still, we were happy that my father could see his grandchildren grow every day and that we could keep an eye on him.

After my mother died, life as we had known it was never the same. My sister, Frida, got married and moved out, leaving my father all alone. We often visited Uncle Shiko and Aunt Regina. During the summer, we went to the beach together every weekend. Adam would drive back and forth many times on his motorcycle and bring everyone to the beach. My cousins Eli and Hanoch were happy children and we had fun together building tents on the beach and having picnics. We had always been a close family, but my mother's death brought us even closer together.

In 1967, we were faced with another war when the Six-Day War broke out in Israel. On the morning of June 5, Adam sent me and the children, Barbara, age eight, and Iris, two, to join our neighbours in the basement shelter of our building. All the men were mobilized. Adam and I had been through so much and now we were to be separated as he went to fulfill his duties in the army. My sister, who was pregnant with her first baby, came to stay with us in the shelter while her husband was away.

The sirens took me back immediately to my childhood and the war. I was petrified and shook constantly. Frida cried that her baby would never know its father and I cried that my children, especially Iris, would not even remember Adam. My own father was in a state of total anguish and would not go into the shelter. He repeated the same phrase over and over. "I have already been in hiding once in my life and I will not go into hiding again. Whatever will happen, will happen."

I was terribly worried about Adam. I heard conflicting stories on my transistor radio. The Israeli station said we were winning the war and the Arabic station said they were winning and would kill all the Israelis and throw them into the sea. All the women and children in the shelter were devastated and united by fear; we shared our terror and hope.

Luckily, the war lasted only six days. Frida's husband, Moshe Palachi, came home soon after, but for sixty days after the war I did not hear a word from Adam. Many of my neighbours had been notified that a family member had been killed or wounded. I comforted myself with the thought that no news was good news. In the meantime, I was working very hard in the overcrowded hospital. My children, terrified and traumatized, spent most of their time playing in the shelter. My father visited me every day and we sat together and worried.

About two months into Adam's silent departure, the doorbell rang and I opened the door to a female officer. I could only think that my husband was dead and immediately fainted. When I finally came to, the woman assured me that Adam was fine. She had been in the same military unit as he was and he had asked her to tell me that he would be home soon and that he sent his love. My father was grateful that his two sons-in-law had survived the war, but he was already working on a plan.

When Adam came home, my father began to talk to us about immigrating to Canada. Every evening the three of us would sit and discuss our future. My father would say, "Adam, you are a young man and have been through so much in your childhood. You are the only surviving member of your family and you have, thank God, survived the Six-Day War. This is a sign that it is your duty to continue your family and your roots. If you stay here, you expose yourself to more wars and danger. Your life is very precious now that you are the head of a family."

I did not want to be separated from my father. "We cannot leave you alone. How can I not be near you?" I cried. My father listened to every word and then continued, "I feel you should go. The best place for you is Canada. You have an aunt, an uncle and a cousin there. They will help sponsor you."

It was a very difficult decision for us to make, one that we knew would dictate our future and that of our children. In a way, I wanted to leave this unsafe and unpredictable place. I didn't want my children to go through wars, as Adam and I had. On the other hand, I didn't have the heart to leave my father. He was too precious to me. I was still suffering the loss of my mother and could not conceive of losing him too. He would not consider coming with us. "Don't worry," he told me, "you will always have a home here with me."

Always the one to play it safe, he did not want us to burn all our bridges at once. We were so confused, deciding one day to leave and changing our minds the next day. Still, my father pushed us. "When you are established in Canada, your sister will join you and, maybe then, I will come. Then we will all be together again."

The most frightening thing for Adam and me was that we would have to start our lives over again in a brand-new country. We had finally mastered Hebrew and now we would need to learn a new language, English. Finally, relentlessly, my father convinced us and we applied to immigrate to Canada. Aunt Mina had written us beautiful letters promising to sponsor us and we went about the business of getting ready to move.

When we applied for our Israeli passports, my mind went back to when we had taken out our Polish passports, where our citizenship had been listed as "not established." Even though we had been born in Poland, like our grandparents and many generations of our families before them, and had suffered through the Holocaust, we were not considered citizens of Poland because we were Jews. It was incomprehensible to me. I still have our Polish passports and once in a while I look at them with disbelief and great regret. This time it was different. We belonged. We were citizens of the State of Israel.

～

In the beginning of 1968, when my father was sixty-one, Shiko and some friends introduced him to a woman. We were still in Israel then and he took me and Adam for a walk. "I have met someone," he told us. "She is a widow, ten years younger than I am. She has two married sons and grandchildren. She has made a very good impression on me and reminds me of your mother. I want you to meet her before I make any commitments."

I could not blame him for not wanting to be alone, even though the thought of someone taking my mother's place made my heart ache. Sara (strangely, she had the same name as my mother) had light-brown curly hair, blue eyes and a friendly personality. I had a very hard time adjusting to another woman in my father's life, but she was good to him and I had no choice but to accept reality. "Dad," I told him, "if she makes you happy, it will make me happy."

The idea that he had someone also made it easier for me to leave Israel. It would have been difficult for me to live near my father and see him with a strange woman at his side. It would be easier to bear in a country far away. We continued with our plans to leave and my father made plans to be married in June.

~

Before our departure for Canada, I decided to sell my violin. We had a limitation on the luggage we could carry and I thought mainly of the many difficulties we would encounter in a new country. With new jobs, learning to speak English and arranging for our children's school and care, I wasn't interested in the violin. The thought of selling the violin frightened me, but I felt we had no choice.

I didn't want to tell my father because I knew he would be furious. It was the only thing I had left of his brother, Velvel. He had given the violin to me, keeping for himself only the kilim rug that Velvel had made with his own hands and had used to wrap the violin when he buried it.

The man at the music shop offered very little for it. I knew it was worth a lot of money, but the man would not budge on his price. Adam, angry and shocked, said to him, "I would rather burn this violin than sell it to you." He grabbed the violin from the man's hand and we left the shop at once. I was relieved and I suddenly realized how happy I was to still have the violin in my possession. What could I have been thinking to want to sell it?

"Let's leave the violin with my father," I told Adam, "and we will be able to get it from him later." I felt that it was fate that had stopped us from selling this precious piece of my history – that I was meant to have it. I vowed I would never again lose my inheritance from Velvel. Thank God my father never knew about our foolish plan. He agreed to keep the violin for me as long as necessary. Even after the violin was safely with my father, I was still nervous just thinking that in a split second I might have lost it. It had been hidden from the Nazis, buried in the ground during the Holocaust, as I had been. In its case we had found the baby pictures that Velvel had wanted me to have. I knew this violin had a story to tell.

Part Five: Canada

Chapter 28

The day arrived when we said our goodbyes and made our way to the unknown. We arrived at Toronto International Airport on September 7, 1968. Aunt Mina, Uncle Moses, Luci and her husband, Abraham, were all there to greet us at the airport with flowers. It was good to see my family. Their home would be our home for just a short while. Soon, we rented a place of our own, found a school for Barbara, who was nine at the time, and a nursery school for Iris, who was three.

Within two weeks of our arrival in Toronto, I had a wonderful job as a scientist with a research team at the Public Health Laboratory in the Ministry of Health. All my diplomas and qualifications from Israel were recognized. I worked in the bacteriology department doing research in the field of gonorrhea. Adam found work at the Douglas Aircraft facility.

We settled into our new life. Our daughters were growing and doing well in school, Adam was happy in his work and I was flourishing in mine. Many of my scientific papers were published in medical and scientific journals. I corresponded with scientists from all over the world, who often asked me for reprints of my work. I lectured and found that scientists paid attention to my findings with great interest and asked for my advice. Finally, I felt fulfilled. After five years, we became Canadian citizens. We were very proud and happy. Now we had a permanent home. Canada was our country and we would never emigrate again. It was truly the best place to live.

In 1973, my father brought his new wife to visit. It was hard for me, but gradually we became friends. During their three-month visit, my children renewed their relationship with their grandfather and he enjoyed being with them. He was happy to see how we had settled into our new home and that we were living a rich and productive life. I was happy to see that he was no longer alone and had found companionship.

During the weekdays, as Adam and I worked, my father busied himself establishing a fruit-and-flower garden in the backyard of the small, semi-detached house we had just bought. I loved that he planted peonies because they reminded me of Bubbie Frida's garden in Turka, and sour cherry trees because they had been my mother's favourite. By the time he left, my garden was beautiful. It was planted with his taste and his choices. He was the specialist and we let him do whatever he wanted. It brought back memories of my earliest childhood for both my father and me.

On weekends, we went to a trailer park in the countryside near Stouffville, outside Toronto, where Adam and I had a small house trailer. We enjoyed our time outdoors very much. My father, coming from a farm as he did, loved this kind of life. He would wake early to enjoy the fresh air, listen to the birds sing and look at the beautiful maple trees. We went to the farmer's market in Stouffville and bought fresh produce and the freshly-baked country bread they sold there.

Before he left, my father asked me to sponsor my sister and her family. In 1975, we welcomed Frida, Moshe and their children to Canada. My father would have gladly joined us here in Canada but his new wife, Sara, did not want to be separated from her two sons and grandchildren in Israel. When my father left Canada, I missed him terribly. I missed his serene smile and his cheerful disposition. I was sorry there was such a great distance separating us.

During his stay with us, my father had become friendly with our neighbour, Mr. Noble, who was his age and also originally from Poland. They often had long enjoyable conversations together. Sometime later, Mr. Noble told me he was going to Israel and asked for my father's address. My father asked him to bring back the violin I had left in his care. At first Mr. Noble refused, but my father insisted, and when the Nobles returned from their trip, he came to see me with my violin in his hand. It seemed that fate, again, had brought the violin back to me.

~

All the pieces of my life were finally coming together. The past was far away and the years were progressing. In 1977, Adam and I celebrated our twenty-first wedding anniversary. It was a beautiful summer evening and I was excited that one of my scientific papers had just been accepted for publication. As I entered the house, exhausted from the long drive home from work, I looked forward to a relaxing bath. Both our daughters had made plans for the evening and Adam would soon be home. We could share a relaxing evening at home, just the two of us. I turned on the stereo and glanced towards the dining room. There, on the dining room table, was a beautiful arrangement of red roses. Their deep red colour and sweet smell filled the room. I read the card from Adam again and again. At this moment, I realized I was the luckiest and happiest woman in the world. I had a loving and wonderful husband, two wonderful daughters, a beautiful, warm home and an exciting career. This was a life most women dream about and for me it had seemed unreachable. I never imagined I would survive past my tenth birthday, let alone live to have such a fulfilling and secure life.

My thoughts were suddenly interrupted by the telephone. It was our friend Jadzia, whom we had met in Canada, but who was also from Poland. She knew many of the people we had known in Poland and was organizing a reunion of people from my Jewish school in Wrocław. She was calling to make sure that we would be there. "Who else is coming?" I asked excitedly. She answered cautiously, "I won't tell you. It'll be a surprise."

Now I was really curious. I went to the full-length mirror in the hall to look at myself. It was one of my favourite things to do. It might sound vain, but I needed mirrors everywhere. It started from my childhood and the way I loved to look at myself in the water of our well. I could not pass by a mirror without looking into it and, most of the time, was not even aware that I was staring into it. When I looked at myself in the mirror, I felt alive. It confirmed that I existed.

I stood in front of the mirror and looked at my face. It was smooth and had no signs of wrinkles. My eyelashes were still thick and long. My hair was light brown with no signs of grey yet. I felt young. Adam had been a very caring husband and father, and we loved each other as deeply as we had when we first met. We were secure in the knowledge that I was his world and he was mine. We never grew tired of or were bored with each other. We were always together, sharing every moment in happiness and joy. I walked slowly to the bedroom and rested my eyes on our wedding portrait hanging over our bed. Adam had not changed much over the years. He had been such a handsome groom. His wonderful smile still showed off his beautiful lips and his straight white teeth. Most of all I loved his eyes. Even now he had thick, black eyebrows accenting his large brown eyes. Loving and warm, they spoke of his honesty, steadfastness and endless love.

~

When the day of the reunion arrived, I was very excited. I had been thinking about it all day. I tried on several outfits and eventually chose my forest-green silk dress that flared at the bottom. The green would go very well, I decided, with my tanned complexion and my light-brown hair arranged in a bun with a fresh coral rose pinned beside it. I did not wear a lot of makeup but I was very fond of fine gold jewellery. I decided on my gold necklace with the diamond pendant and matching earrings. Adam wore his favourite navy blue suit with a white shirt and tie to match.

When we arrived at Jadzia's house, there were many cars already parked on both sides of the road and I hoped we were not the last to arrive. Suddenly, I felt shaky. "Maybe we should go home," I whispered to Adam, unsure why I was feeling that way. "Don't be nervous," he told me, pulling me closer to him. "You look gorgeous. Everyone will be jealous of my beautiful wife." He rang the doorbell and soon Jadzia stood smiling in the open entrance. "Everybody's waiting for you downstairs. Come on in."

I was still trembling a little as the loud noise hit my ears. As we walked into the party room, conversation stopped and everyone looked at us. I held on tightly to Adam's hand and looked around. He whispered that he was going to get us a drink from the bar and as I stood alone I looked around the room again, wondering who the surprise guest was.

Suddenly I noticed an older man, a drink in his hand, observing me. When our eyes met, he moved toward me, smiling. At once I recognized those eyes, but was overcome with amazement when I looked into them. They did not seem to go with the grey curly hair and the wrinkled skin of his face. I felt weak and the room suddenly lacked air.

"Rachel," Peter said, as he put his arms around my neck and kissed me. I was motionless. Suddenly, I was back into the far past. Had it really been twenty-four years since our last goodbye? Adam saw me talking to Peter and kept his distance while Peter told me what had really happened all those years ago. His mother had insisted that I wouldn't be able to have children because I was so small. She gave him an ultimatum. It was to be either his mother or me. He had chosen his mother. He told me that he knew now how stupid he had been and how much he had suffered for his stupidity. Since our breakup he could not stand to be with his mother.

"When I gave you up," he told me, "she lost me anyway." He was married and had children, he told me, but he was unhappy. He still dreamed about me. I looked at him sadly and said quietly, "I am very happily married and have two beautiful daughters and a lovely home.

I don't believe we were meant to be together. You know I believe in fate. Sometimes we chase our own luck away. But I have no regrets. I love my husband and I know he loves me very much." I was choking back tears as I spoke because it was so obvious that his dreams had not come true – that he was left with a broken heart. I felt terribly sorry for him. At that moment, Adam approached us and asked me to dance with him. The music was lively. I was in Adam's arms, exactly where I was supposed to be.

That chapter of my life was closed. I felt free to carry on with my work and family life. I had become interested in belly dancing and was taking lessons. I loved the colourful costumes, which reminded me of the Gypsies dancing in Turka when I was a little girl. When I was belly dancing, I entered a whole new world. I learned how to make my own colourful costumes and was proud to perform for my husband. We began going to Middle Eastern restaurants to watch the professional belly dancers. When I became more advanced, I would surprise my friends at their birthday parties. I always had my little red cassette player with me and my Middle Eastern music tape. They couldn't believe I had chosen belly dancing as a hobby. It was so different from my profession and my life. For me, dancing was a private part of my life that I kept separate from my colleagues. Doing a beautiful veil dance that I had designed myself brought back memories of my childhood. I remembered the first pair of shoes my father had bought for me after the war. When he had asked me if they were comfortable, I answered, "I don't know yet. First I have to dance in them and then I will be able to tell." I remember how I danced all over the store, not at all embarrassed. Perhaps I did have some Gypsy blood in me after all.

Chapter 29

I visited my father in Israel every year. These visits were very precious to me. I loved the feeling of being, once again, daddy's little girl. The distance between my childhood and my life as a grown woman would disappear as my father held my hand when we crossed the street, or at mealtimes when he constantly refilled my plate. As soon as my head was turned, he would pile more food on my plate. Humouring him, I would act surprised and say, "Dad, I don't remember having so much food on my plate. What happened?" He would look at me calmly and say, "I don't know. Just eat it all up." At those moments we could have been in Turka or Wrocław, when my well-being and happiness were of utmost importance to him. He was so sweet and adorable in my eyes, I could never get mad at his deep concern for me.

We had very good times together. We played chess and went for walks, though they had to be short ones. He had been a heavy smoker since he was very young and no matter how much I begged him, he did not stop smoking even though he now suffered from emphysema. At the end of my visits, we would cry as if it were our last time together.

His health began deteriorating very rapidly. When my daughter Barbara was married in June 1981, my father could not attend her wedding. In December, I received a call that my father was very sick and in hospital. I immediately flew to Israel, trembling and praying all the way that I would still find him alive. I could not imagine living without him. He was so wise. I had always depended on him for advice and direction. When I arrived at the hospital, he was very much alive and his blue eyes lit up when he saw me. I knew that just seeing me made him feel better. For three weeks, I spent my days and nights at the hospital by his side. He was so beautiful in my eyes. He had no wrinkles and not a single grey hair. He had always looked younger than his age. He would be turning seventy-five in January. It broke my heart to think that he had had such a hard life and now, when his life was peaceful, his time was running out. How I wanted to help him! But it was not in my hands. With great hope for his improvement, I returned home when my father was released from the hospital. On January 8, 1982, I called to wish him happy birthday, but he was not at home. He was back in the hospital, where he passed away a few days later.

The pain of the loss of my father was unbearable. Lonely and lost, I felt like a small child again. How unfair it was that both of my parents had died so young. After surviving the horrors of the Holocaust, they deserved, at least, the compensation of a long and healthy life.

Shiko was also in very poor emotional shape. They had been such close brothers, always together through the bad and good times, and one could not live without the other. Now, Shiko, too, was alone. He became very depressed and told me many times that he would not live long and would soon die. I felt furious when he said this and tried to cheer him up.

In one telephone conversation I told him, "Shiko, please take care of yourself. You know that now that I have lost my father, you must be both my uncle and my father." He was silent. Frightened that something had happened to him, I screamed his name into the receiver, but he did not answer. "What has happened to you?" I shouted. "Have I said something wrong? Are you alright?" Finally, after a long while, he slowly began to speak again. When I asked Adam if he thought I had been wrong to suggest that he would now be both an uncle and a father to me, he could not imagine that it would offend him. I never mentioned this incident to Shiko again.

Chapter 30

Adam and I had a great deal to celebrate in the years after my father's death. Both of our daughters graduated from university – Barbara with a degree in chemistry and biochemistry, and Iris with a degree in nutrition and food sciences. Our daughter Barbara gave birth to beautiful twin girls, Shari, named after my mother, Sara, and Julie, named after her father's great-grandmother. The babies became my whole life. My world revolved around them and my own Bubbie Frida's voice rang in my ears as I told them what she had told me. "You are my life and my world." I was sorry that my father had not lived to see his great-granddaughters. I also knew that if it weren't for those two babies, I would not have been able to get over his death. Two years after my father's death, Shiko died of lung cancer. He was only seventy-one.

Years passed and Barbara had another beautiful daughter, Ashley, named after Adam's grandmother, Esther. Iris got married and had two gorgeous girls a year apart. Sophie was named for her father's grandmother and Elisse for my father, Israel. Adam and I were now the proud grandparents of five granddaughters. With our children all grown up and their lives settled and moving forward, Adam suggested we take early retirement. "Life is short," he told me, "we should enjoy ourselves. Now we can travel, relax and enjoy our hobbies." In 1988, I took early retirement at the age of fifty-three. I decided to enjoy every moment. I spent time on my home and devoted more time to belly dancing and exercise. We bought a van, which Adam customized with a sofa bed, a small table, a bench where we could sit together or another person could sleep, and a small sink. We were all set for the road. Eventually, we outgrew our van and decided to pull our thirty-foot trailer behind us. Now we had space for everyone. Time started to move too quickly and the years went by unnoticed.

In 1993, when I was fifty-eight years old, I came to a turning point in my life – a turning point sparked by a chance remark.

~

Our daughter Iris had invited Barbara's family and Frida's family for a farewell dinner for us before our annual trip to Florida. It was a wonderful evening and when dessert and coffee were being served, Sarit, Frida's daughter, began an interesting discussion. She was talking about the colour of Iris's eyes compared to her children's eyes. "How come you have brown eyes," she asked Iris, "and your husband has brown eyes, but Elisse has blue eyes?"

Iris explained to her that brown-eyed parents can have children with eyes of any colour because brown is a dominant colour, but that blue-eyed parents, who have a recessive gene, cannot have brown-eyed children. Sarit looked at her mother's eyes and then at my eyes and said in surprise, "But our grandparents had blue and green eyes and my mother has green eyes, but your mother has brown eyes. How can that be?" Iris looked at her and jokingly said, "Because my mother is not their real daughter." Everyone at the table laughed. Her answer, meant in jest, had caught me by surprise. I began to drift away from the conversation and my life unfolded before my eyes. In shock, I thought about my parents, Frida and myself. We were a family. How could it be otherwise? Distressed, I could not sleep that night, my head spinning out of control with the implications of what an innocent conversation had unleashed.

The next morning, I began to look for evidence. I opened my immunology and serology book and looked up the different blood types. I knew that my mother's had been AB, my father was B and I was type O. In black and white, the truth stared me in the face. "A type AB mother cannot have a type O child." Even though I had studied medicine and knew all of this information as a matter of fact, I had never applied it to myself. Why would I question my origins?

It was as though in those few moments alone with a book of science, I lost myself. Who was I? I could not believe how this kind of secret could have been kept from me all of these years. At age fifty-eight, with both of my parents gone, I was faced with a lifetime of questions and no one to answer them.

I immediately went to the doctor to have my blood type rechecked. My suspicions were confirmed. My parents had not been my biological parents. How could I cope with this sudden reality? My world collapsed. I was rootless. Why had no one in my family been honest with me in all these years and told me of my true origins? I loved them all so much, how could this be happening to me? I had been so rich, blessed with wonderful parents and a warm and loving family. Now, I was as alone as a stone – a true equal to Adam, who had lost his parents and family in the war and was so lonely until our marriage. But there was a difference between us. He remembered his parents. Their faces and names. He knew where he was born and to whom. I did not know anything of my true history. I was a lost child. Now I would be mourning two sets of parents, the ones I knew and loved and the ones who were faceless and a mystery to me.

I could no longer function and became very depressed. I went into therapy. I had no interest in my life or surroundings and became preoccupied with trying to find answers to my new identity. Adam tried very hard to drag me out of seclusion. I could not sleep and dreaded each new day that seemed to lead only to more questions. This was a wound I could not bear; I believed I would never get over it. I could rely only on Adam, who never left my side, and my children. How would I ever forgive my parents? Not because they were not my biological parents, but because they had not told me the truth.

My entire life had been a lie. After weeks of torment, I decided to turn to the few remaining members of my family for answers. I asked them all, "Who were my biological parents?" They listened politely and shook their heads. I turned to Aunt Mina. "A mother that raises you is not a mother?" my mother's sister asked accusingly. When I tried to explain what I had discovered to her, she still would not admit anything. I was convinced that she had been sworn to secrecy and that by telling me the truth she would be breaking a pact with my mother. Neither my logic nor my pleading helped. She remained silent. When I approached another family member, she became annoyed with me and replied angrily, "Why are you making such a fuss? What difference does it make who your biological mother was?"

I felt deeply hurt and betrayed, but continued to probe. Another family member gave me the same answer. "I do not know anything, but even if I did, I wouldn't tell you." I begged him, "Please tell me the truth. You know I loved my parents, but I am entitled to know where I came from." My heart ached and I was desolate. Every door was slammed in my face. It felt, for the first time in my entire life, as though I had no family or friends at all. As a last resort, I had one more person I could go to. I opened my heart to her and told her everything I was feeling. She treated me even more harshly than the rest. "Your mother suffered so much with you when you were ill and now she is not your mother? You should be ashamed of yourself. Go to both your parents' graves and ask for forgiveness." Then she added, "Do not ever speak of this again."

Turned away by my entire family, I was by then increasingly convinced that I had found the truth anyway. Throughout their lives my parents had talked about the dearest person to them, about Velvel, and his love, Nelly. They did not want me to forget him and his legacy. But they had not told me everything. I was sure that the violin was the key to this unspoken secret, that it alone held the truth. My precious violin would be my best friend and the source of the answers I so desperately needed.

I stopped discussing the matter with my family and began my own investigation. I realized that I had all the pieces of my life's puzzle in my own hands. Still in turmoil and dismay, Adam and I began our annual drive to Florida. Distracted and in pain, I looked into the darkness for a sign, anything to help me in my quest. At one point we stopped for a rest at a plaza on the turnpike. It was very late at night and as Adam went into the building for some coffee, I stayed outside to walk a little and stretch my legs. As I approached the building, I noticed something shiny on the ground. I bent down to have a better look and found it was a gold chain with a golden *chai* (the traditional Jewish symbol for life) on it. At first I felt uneasy about picking it up, but I decided that if I did not take it, someone else would. When Adam came back I showed him what I had found. Back in the trailer, I washed it with soap and told Adam, "This will be my good luck charm. I will always keep it with me because it will be a symbol for me of the Hebrew name given to me at birth, Chai Rachel."

My mind flew to all the pieces of the puzzle. Maybe Velvel was my biological father. I looked like him. My parents kept his memory alive so fervently in me while I was growing up. His violin was given to me and only I was to play it. In the violin case he had placed my baby pictures, pictures of himself and a picture of his cousin Minka with a girlfriend. But who was this girlfriend? An enlargement of Velvel's picture hung over the grand piano in our living room in Wrocław and a picture of me was hung beside it. My parents had spoken often of Velvel and his love affair with Nelly. I went over and over these clues in my head. Velvel must have been my biological father. Nelly must have been my biological mother.

I remembered the letter my mother had written to Nelly after the war telling her that they had survived the war and so had the child. I hadn't paid much attention to that letter back then, but now it seemed so important. My mother had written to Nelly, the girl from Warsaw with whom Velvel had been in love before the war. She wrote Nelly that she, Sara, Israel and the child were alive and had survived the war. Velvel, she added, had not survived. She asked Nelly to write back and to tell her about herself.

My mother told me that Nelly had been very beautiful and had a lovely nature. She said that she had loved Nelly and that they had been the best of friends. She told me that Nelly had been the love of Velvel's life and that she remembered how devastated Velvel was when Zeyde Eli had refused to give his consent to their marriage. Zeyde Eli had already promised Velvel's hand in marriage to his brother Mendel's daughter, Sala, and in Orthodox Judaism this type of promise could not be broken.

At the time, I wondered why my mother was telling me this story. After all, Velvel had died and I did not see the point in talking about him and his love affairs. A short time after my mother sent the letter, a telegram arrived from Warsaw from Nelly's sister. "Nelly is alive," it said, "but dead to the world." We never found out exactly what this meant.

It was so clear to me now. Why would she have written to an old girlfriend of her late brother-in-law? Why would this girl care if we had survived? I remembered how Bubbie Yetta would always call me a fool. Then I could not understand it and it had caused me such pain. She had never called Luci a fool. Now I understood. Of course I was a fool. I did not have a clue as to who I was and who my biological parents were. Luci was her grandchild, I was not.

I thought back to all the times my father had brought up the subject of adopted children. Often he would ask me if I thought adopted children ever felt that something was not right. He must have wanted to see my reaction. I never had any idea what he was talking about. No wonder he had insisted so strongly that I not cut my long braids. Today when I look at the photograph of the pretty girl with long, dark-blond braids in the photograph that Velvel put into the violin case, it matches the description my mother gave me of Nelly. It makes perfect sense that Velvel had wanted me to know the truth and, desperate, knowing that there wasn't much time, put all the clues he could in the violin case.

My conversation with Uncle Shiko came back to me vividly, and how shocked he had been when I referred to him as my uncle and my father. Now I understood it perfectly. He must have been so taken aback by what I said that it left him speechless. Who, he must have wondered, has told her? What a conspiracy it all seemed to me now! How could all these people, people I loved and trusted, have kept this truth from me? No one had thought enough of me to tell me. Now, I would be mourning two sets of parents.

Chapter 31

Once I had put the pieces of my life together and had come to terms with the truth, I was able to find peace. Now I am taking good care of my precious violin. It has helped me to find out who I am and to be proud of my inheritance. If it could speak, it would tell me all of its secrets.

Sometimes my children and I play music together. Barbara plays the piano, Iris the flute and I play my violin. We always play the song Velvel taught me, "Tum-Ba-La-Laika." I have taught my granddaughters to sing this song in Yiddish and hope my legacy will go on. The kilim rug that protected the violin for me is now also in my possession and, made by his own hand, it is a symbol of what Velvel did for me. He wanted me to know the truth about my birth and used his most precious possession, his violin, to do so.

At age fifty-eight, after such a traumatic discovery, I needed an outlet for all I felt. I had a deep urgency to share my discovery with others. At first, I talked to my grandchildren about my history. I was determined to teach them about the Holocaust and about my own childhood. They were very interested in my stories and asked me to write a book about my life. The idea of opening up the memories of the past again frightened me. Did I have the strength to relive the nightmares of my childhood, the horrible experiences of the Holocaust? I carried so much rage inside of me. I could not forget the destruction of my happy childhood, the murder of my loved ones and the uprooting of my family so many times.

In 1996, when Steven Spielberg began his program to videotape the testimonies of Holocaust survivors, I decided that it was now or never; I would tell my story. I had great difficulty convincing Adam that he should tell his special story too, being the only survivor of his family. I wanted our children and grandchildren to remember and the world to know.

We were very fortunate to have a wonderful and exceptional interviewer, Myrna Riback. She approached us with great understanding and compassion. It was with her encouragement that I decided to go ahead and write my story. There were times when I felt like giving up my writing, but Myrna, with her steady support and smiling face, did not give up on me. Once I began writing my story, there was no turning back. I was amazed at how much I remembered about the world that I had tried so hard to forget for so long. The details, the people, the conversations and the places were real and lived vividly in my mind.

Deep in my heart, I know my father is proud of me. I believe he is happy that I have solved the puzzle all by myself. I can see him smiling. He always liked a good detective story.

When I was a young girl in Poland after the war, my father would often go to the courthouse to listen to interesting cases, particularly paternity cases. It became a kind of hobby for him, trying to predict the outcome of a complicated case. He liked solving difficult problems. Many times he would take me with him for company. Perhaps, if my discovery had not come so late, he would have told me the truth.

Epilogue

I have had to adjust to many changes in my life. It restores my sense of self that in the face of these changes – both chosen and forced upon me – I have been able to adapt and grow. The moves to Israel and Canada, the struggle to build a new life, one so different from the world we left behind – all these things were within my ability and only made me stronger. I have preserved the things that were dear to me from the past and I have achieved the goals I set for myself. I intend to enjoy every moment of the rest of my life to the fullest.

I will not take anything for granted. I know better.

The remarkable discovery of who my biological parents were was achieved, not with the help of strangers, but with the love and wisdom of my husband, Adam. He helped me face the events of my life and solve the mystery.

All this time, the violin has held the key. I feel a deep and awesome connection to Velvel and the clues he left for me in his violin case. Velvel and Nelly placed me in very good hands. They knew my biological family would not let me down. Finding out what my roots really were has given me an even greater sense of belonging to my much-adored Milbauer family.

I am deeply grateful for the truly beautiful relationship I had with my father, who was really my uncle. He fulfilled all that Velvel had entrusted to him. He always showed me great love, concern and devotion and never for a moment veered from the promise he had made to his brother.

Today, when I play my violin, I truly feel that I am worthy of the tears of pain and loss, of the unrealized dreams, for which it was the repository.

A Child's Testimony

Testimony of Adam Shtibel (Abram Sztybel)
March 3, 1948

Translated from the original Polish
by Henia and Nochem Reinhartz

Editor's Note

In the immediate aftermath of World War II, the Central Jewish Historical Commission (CJHC) in Warsaw collected thousands of testimonies from Jews who had survived the horrors of the Holocaust as children. Adam Shtibel, then called Abram Sztybel, was one of these children.[1] At the time of his testimony, March 3, 1948, Adam was nineteen years old and living in a student dormitory in Warsaw. With no surviving family and uncertain about his future, Adam remembers that he was hesitant to give his testimony and felt great anxiety at the prospect of having to speak out loud about his experiences.

Adam was interviewed by Genia Silkes, a staff member at the CJHC. Adam's deposition, like the other testimonies collected by the CJHC during this period, was taken down according to a particular methodology developed for child survivors. Using a questionnaire prepared by the staff, an interviewer asked questions and took detailed notes as the child survivor gave his or her testimony. Following the interview, the interviewer wrote up the testimony in the first-

---

1 Abram decided to become "Adam" in 1948, not long after giving his testimony. Left fearful and insecure by his wartime experiences, he felt that Abram was too obviously a Jewish name. Adam changed the spelling of his last name from the Polish "Sztybel" to the English "Shtibel" when he arrived in Canada in 1968.

person voice; it was then read and reviewed by the survivor and, once approved, signed as a true record of his or her experience.[2]

Even at the time, the staff at CJHC understood that their methodology had shortcomings. As the interviewer was required to reformulate and occasionally summarize information given in a testimony, "some unique and personal characteristics of style and language would be lost."[3] The frequent interruptions in the testimonies – required so that the interviewer had enough time to take accurate notes – sometimes changed the flow and rhythm of the narrative and influenced the way memories were relayed. The method employed by the CJHC was followed, however, because it was one of the only ways to allow children to give detailed testimony. At a time when tape recorders were not widely used, all testimony had to be written by hand. Yet many of the child survivors interviewed had not attended school for years, if at all, and could not express themselves in writing.[4] The method employed by the CJHC gave the children the opportunity to verbalize what they remembered at a time when their memories were fresh and to create a record for future generations where no record would have been left otherwise.

The original Polish-language record of Adam's deposition can be found in the archives of the CJHC, now housed at the Jewish Histori-

---

2   Boaz Cohen, "The Children's Voice: Postwar Collection of Testimonies from Child Survivors of the Holocaust," in *Holocaust and Genocide Studies* 21, no. 1 (2007): 73–95. The Central Jewish Historical Commission was one of only a few organizations that collected testimonies from Jewish children in the immediate post-war period.

3   Rachel Auerbach, "Mekorot u'drachim hadashim l'geviyat eduyot" (New ways and methods for taking testimonies), *Yediot Yad Vashem*, no. 2. (July 29, 1954), as quoted in Cohen, 77.

4   Cohen, 77.

cal Institute in Warsaw.[5] Like other testimonies taken by the CJHC
between 1945 and 1948, the original document opens with a covering
form filled in by the interviewer designed to summarize basic facts
about the person giving testimony. For example, in the form covering Adam's testimony, the interviewer noted that Adam was born on
December 1, 1930, in Komarów in the Lublin district. Interestingly,
Adam did not actually know his real birthdate at the time of the 1948
interview, but had tried to reconstruct an approximate date at the end
of the war. He had thought he was about eight years old when the war
started. In 1984, Adam and Rachel contacted the Komarów city hall
and discovered that his actual birthdate was October 21, 1928; he also
discovered his mother's maiden name, Rotberg. Adam's parents were
listed on the form as Chaim and Basia Sztybel. The form also listed
the places that Adam had lived before and during the war: Komarów,
the village of Wolice, the Zamość forest, Siedlce and the village of
Borki (located in the rural commune of Wodynie in the district of
Siedlce). In the section of the form entitled "concentration camps,"
the interviewer noted that Adam had been interned in Zamość. As
Adam's testimony makes clear, however, the camp in Zamość was actually for internally displaced Poles and not a concentration camp.
The interviewer noted that Adam had attended school until the second grade, but not at all during the war, and that he was able to read
and write some Polish. At the time of the interview, Adam was enrolled in a public school for adult learners.

In the pages that follow, Adam's 1948 testimony is presented in full
in English as translated by Henia and Nochem Reinhartz in 2007. The
tone and cadence of Adam's words are very much that of interview-

---

5   Archive of the Jewish Historical Institute, Warsaw, Testimony of Abram Sztybel,
1948, file no. 3683, in collection 301: *Testimonies of Survivors*. A copy of all the testimonies in collection 301 is also available at the Yad Vashem Archive, Jerusalem,
M49e division.

based testimony. While it is a straightforward account, it lacks extensive explanation or contextualization. Adam's words are also those of a teenager who felt intensely uncomfortable revealing himself and who was recounting events that had happened to him between the ages of ten and sixteen. At that age, it is not surprising that, while Adam is clear about what he witnessed, he is unable to give exact dates. And though he certainly knew that the German authority figures he encountered had the power of life and death over him, he was not able to specifically identify these individuals as Gestapo, army soldiers or police officers. Such issues can make the reading of testimony a more demanding endeavour than the reading of narrative memoir. Great care was taken while preparing the English text of the 1948 document for publication to maintain its integrity as an accurate record of Adam's testimony as taken down by the CJHC.

Several editorial decisions were made while preparing the English text in keeping with our approach to the testimony as an historical document rather than a composed narrative. First, the translated text was lightly edited for grammar and syntax and not at all for style and word choice. When a place or proper name is spelled incorrectly in the original record, the word was left as it was and a footnote has been included with an explanation and correction. Second, when it was felt that phrases or words might require clarification for the English-speaking reader, these clarifications were inserted into the text and shown in square brackets [ ]. In this way, text inserted by the editor is always differentiated from the original testimony. It should be noted that the original Polish text contains text found in round parentheses ( ) and that this text was translated into English in the same way. Third, if it was felt that the reader would benefit from contextual or more extensive historical information, this material is provided in footnotes written by the editor. There are no footnotes in the original Polish-language document.

Finally, this text contains footnotes that were added at the request of Adam Shtibel. In the late 1990s, when Adam Shtibel reviewed the

Polish text for the first time since 1948, he realized that he had not mentioned certain events and people at the time of his deposition. Remembering them a half-century later, he felt strongly that they should be included and recorded as part of his legacy. Rather than including these anecdotes in the text and taking care to differentiate between Adam's 1948 testimony and his more recent memories, these recollections are included in the footnotes.

Naomi Azrieli
Toronto, Ontario
August 2007

A Child's Testimony

Before the war, the little town of Komarów was mostly populated by Jews. It had only a few Polish families. In the centre of town there was a marketplace and around it about fifteen streets. Every Monday there was a fair in the marketplace. The Jews were traders; some owned stores and workshops. There were about 4,000 people in the town.

In Komarów there was a public school that went to Grade 7, and one *kheyder* [Hebrew elementary school][1] where we learned to say prayers and to write Hebrew and Yiddish.

Before the war, we were quite well off. My father sewed for the farmers and my mother sold kerchiefs and fabrics for dresses in the villages. There were four of us in the family. We lived in a wooden house, which was somewhat simple, but we lived well.

When the war broke out, I was eight years old.[2] I attended school and played with other children. The war did not affect us. The Russian army marched into our town.[3] They immediately disarmed the Polish soldiers. The Polish commander committed suicide on the spot.

---

1 All text shown in square parenthesis [ ] has been inserted by the editor and does not appear in the original transcription of Adam's 1948 testimony.

2 As explained in the Editor's Note, Adam did not know until 1984 that in fact he was ten years old at the start of World War II.

3 On September 28, 1939.

The Russians stayed for just two weeks. After two weeks, the Russians retreated and the Germans came in.[4] The Russians had been received by the town with applause and flowers. The town was sad when the Russians prepared to leave. The Russians provided trucks and announced that people who wanted to could go to Russia with them.

We intended to leave, but unfortunately it was a Saturday, *Shabbes*, and my mother was religious so we stayed put. After that it was already too late as the Germans marched in and everything changed. They began beating Jews for no reason at all. They confiscated goods in the stores and looted homes. They grabbed Jews to do dirty work. The Germans ordered Jews to register for work during Rosh Hashanah [the Jewish New Year], so many Jews did not register because of the holiday. The Jews who did not register were taken by the Germans and sent to a camp in Laszczów; this was a labour camp.[5] My brother

---

4   Under the terms of the Nazi-Soviet Non-aggression Treaty signed in August 1939, Poland was divided between Germany and the USSR. The town of Komarów was situated close to the new dividing line in Poland and came under fluctuating German and Soviet occupation in the early weeks of the war. Thus, on September 13, 1939, Komarów was occupied by the German army. On September 28, 1939, the Germans withdrew and were replaced by the Red Army. Soviet units remained in Komarów for two weeks, awaiting the outcome of German-Soviet negotiations on the final territorial division of Poland. On October 10, 1939, the Germans returned, after which Komarów and the surrounding areas remained fully under German control until mid-1944. *Pinkas Hakehillot Polin* (Encyclopaedia of the Jewish Communities of Poland), ed. Abraham Wein, vol. 7, *Lublin and Kielce Districts* (Jerusalem: Yad Vashem, 1999), 467–468.

5   The first German occupation of Komarów occurred on the eve of the Jewish New Year, September 13, 1939. The labour conscriptions described here by Adam were initiated shortly after the second German occupation, which commenced on October 10, 1939. *Pinkas Hakehillot Polin*, 467. The German authorities set up an elaborate system of camps throughout occupied Poland that were designated for various populations, such as POWs, Jews, Poles, or for the purpose of organizing population transfers, forced labour, or genocide. Dieter Pohl, "War, Occupation,

was sent to that camp. The Germans came to our house and ordered him to get dressed in ten minutes. When my brother had been in the camp for two months, he became sick with typhus and was sent home. We called a doctor and he took care of him. My brother remained at home and began learning the tailoring trade with a neighbour.

We were only allowed to be outside until eight o'clock in the evening. Jews could no longer go to the villages [outside of Komarów] to trade. We had to wear a white armband with a Star of David. We were punished for the smallest things. Once our neighbour went to the synagogue without the armband and the Germans killed him on the spot. There was one Gestapo man called Ne.[6] He was a mean killer who was always looking for an opportunity to torture Jews. Our town had a *shoykhet*, an elderly man who slaughtered geese and chickens for our town.[7] When the Germans heard about him, they found him and took him to the centre. They gave him a terrible beating, pulling at his beard, kicking him, and [then they] took him to prison in

---

and the Holocaust in Poland," in *The Historiography of the Holocaust*, ed. Dan Stone (New York: Palgrave, 2004), 96–97. Laszczów is located approximately twenty-five kilometres south-east of Komarów.

6 The German authorities dispatched many different police and security forces to occupied Poland, including military police, the Gestapo (the State political police), the Order Police (regular uniformed German police) and others. Adam, eleven years old at the time, knew that Ne was a high-ranking police officer, but did not know what kind, referring to him in two ways during his 1948 testimony: here, as a "Gestapo man" and on page 184 as a "German policeman."

7 Observant Jews follow a system of rules known as *kashruth*, or kosher dietary laws. These rules regulate what observant Jews eat, how food is prepared and how meat and poultry are slaughtered. A *shoykhet* is a man conversant with the relevant religious teachings who is trained to slaughter animals painlessly and check the meat afterward to be sure it meets the various criteria of *kashruth*. Anita Diamant, *Living a Jewish Life* (New York: Harper Collins, 1991), 95–97. For more information, see the glossary.

Zamość.[8] They also arrested the families who owned the geese and chickens that the *shoykhet* had slaughtered. Our *shoykhet* was tortured and starved so terribly in prison that he died, leaving behind his family.

Soon the Germans prohibited us from wearing furs, sheepskin coats and fur collars. Everything had to be taken to the square and handed over to the Germans. We did not give up our sheepskin coats, but buried them in a cubby-hole under the house. Nobody saw it and nobody knew about it. Later, we were threatened with death if we wore furs. One woman, who was new in town, crossed the street wearing a fur collar and the Germans killed her. Fear spread throughout our town.

The town had a committee composed of the wealthier Jews.[9] Every month we received ration cards for sugar, salt, flour and other products – one quarter of a kilo per person. My father worked at his trade and my mother traded food illegally. My brother also worked as a tailor.

Jews from the surrounding villages and towns were resettled into

---

8   Zamość was the major town and administrative centre of the district. Before the war, it had a population of approximately 24,000, of which more than 10,000 were estimated to be Jewish. Zamość had a long history as a vibrant centre of Jewish life before the war. *Pinkas Hakehillot Polin*, op cit., pp. 203–212. Zamość is located approximately twenty kilometres from Komarów.

9   Committees like the one described here were formed in most Jewish communities in Poland following the German occupation. Consisting of local Jewish community leaders appointed by the Germans, these committees were charged with communicating and carrying out German edicts and regulations, and also with the care of displaced and destitute Jews. Doris L. Bergen, *War and Genocide: A Concise History of the Holocaust* (Toronto: Rowman & Littlefield, 2003), 114. On the Komarów committee, see *Pinkas Hakehillot Polin*, 467.

Komarów.[10] These people were terribly poor; they did not have anything to eat and had nowhere to stay. At first, they lived in the synagogues. The committee took care of them. Slowly, they were placed in people's houses; every Jew had to take in a family of deportees. The committee organized a soup kitchen for them where they got soup every day. There was no nursery school for the children, no soup kitchen. The children's food came from the same kitchen as the adults'.

The young men and adults signed up to work for the Germans. Every morning a truck took them to Zamość and brought them back in the evening. Later, the Germans began to round up Jews for work sending them to a [labour] camp in Zamość.

I attended *kheyder*. The *kheyder* was illegal and only about twenty boys attended it. We studied all day, but only until noon on Fridays. The rabbi had two sons. One was fifteen years old, the other sixteen. They had to help their parents and sold cigarettes and matches. We stayed in *kheyder* until five o'clock. Only the wealthier children attended *kheyder*, those whose parents could afford to pay. At first, I did not know that the Germans were bad. I only heard people talk about it. I only learned once the Germans occupied our town.[11]

---

10 Soon after the consolidation of the occupation in Poland, German authorities embarked on a policy of forcibly resettling Jews into towns and urban areas. This policy culminated in the establishment of ghettos, when a section of a town or city was closed off and severe restrictions on movement and outside communication were applied. As Adam witnessed first-hand, prior to the official establishment of the ghetto, Komarów experienced several influxes of people, including a spring 1941 influx of seven hundred Jews from as far away as Czechoslovakia. Bergen, 111; *Pinkas Hakehillot Polin*, 467.

11 In text placed at the very end of Adam's 1948 deposition, he said, "Back when I was still in *kheyder*, we used to play a game pretending to be Germans. We took the rabbi's shovels, sticks and pokers and ran through the courtyards screaming in German and [pretending to be] chasing Jews, 'Heraus! verfluchter Hund! Jude!' [Get out! You damn dog! Jew!] The neighbours would yell at us that we sounded crazy, we answered them in German."

Our little town had no orphanage. Poor children begged or traded. They took soap, matches, cigarettes and other things to farmers [outside of town]. The farmers paid them with food: potatoes, flour, cereals and lard. The older people could not trade because the Germans did not permit it. Little children, however, could get through various passages more easily. The Polish police and the German military police patrolled the roads and the villages [surrounding Komarów] and if they caught a Jewish child they beat him up and took away his wares. For entertainment, they [the police] often chased the children so that they would spill their wares. The children would return home with nothing. Polish children often called [them] names like "scabby Jew," laughed at them and harassed them.

There were no books to read. When we returned home from *kheyder*, we played with sleighs, we skated and so on. Our relatives lived in Komarów and in Tomaszów.[12] We lived without their help and they lived without our help. My brother and I liked to listen to the adults' conversations about how the war would soon end, about events in our town, and news about the war. I would listen to their conversations about the fate of the Jews. I was upset by what I heard. My brother and I, along with our friends, talked about how we needed to know what to do. On our way home from *kheyder*, my friends and I discussed what the grownups were saying and we worried about how bad things were for us.

Many Komarów children left to work as shepherds for the farmers [in nearby villages]. At home, there was hunger, but at the farmers' in the villages there was always some food. Sometimes there was even food to take home. Many Jewish children worked for farmers. At the time, the farmers were quite willing to take on Jewish children

---

12 Tomaszów was a town of similar size to Komarów located approximately thirty kilometres to the south.

because a Jewish farmhand worked a lot and did not demand much.

The summer of 1941 was very hot. The Germans designated a quarter where Jews were allowed to live – all the streets to the right of the marketplace.[13] We were not allowed to leave. Polish police patrolled the roads. A person caught leaving the ghetto risked imprisonment. There was less and less food and the hunger was great. It was very crowded. Everybody was forced to live in these few streets. Several families had to live in one house. In our house, too, there were three strangers besides our family.

Typhus spread in our little town. Almost every home became infected. The Jewish police searched every home looking for the ill.[14] The sick people were put on a cart and taken to the Jewish community hospital. My father got sick with typhus. They took him to the hospital. We were not allowed to visit, we were only allowed to come to the gate. The medical care was very poor and so was the food. They gave the patients black bread and black coffee even though the sick

---

13 The Komarów ghetto was established in June 1941. This was the final stage of the process of isolation and concentration that began in the autumn of 1939 with forced resettlements of Jews from elsewhere into the town. *Pinkas Hakehillot Polin*, 467.

14 Once a ghetto was established, the Germans appointed a Jewish Council (Judenrat) to administer the Jewish population and carry out German orders. In order to fulfill their role as community leaders and uphold order in the ghetto, the councils were assisted by a Jewish police force. The councils appeared to be self-governing entities, but they were under complete German control. There has been much debate and controversy surrounding the role of the Jewish Councils and the Jewish police in the deportation and eventual murder of the Jews incarcerated in ghettos. While many individuals, especially in the Jewish police, have been held up to harsh criticism, recent research has shown that many Jewish Councils worked to help their fellow Jews under extraordinarily difficult and arbitrary circumstances. Bergen, 114; Tim Cole, "Ghettoization," in *The Historiography of the Holocaust*, 70–72; Michael Marrus, *The Holocaust in History* (New York: Penguin, 1993), 113–120.

ones had fevers of over 40°C and could not eat the food. Each home with a sick person was disinfected. Everything was taken out into the backyard and a yellow powder was sprinkled in the home. The smell of the powder was so strong that afterward it was impossible to stay indoors. Father was in the hospital for three weeks. They kept saying that his condition was improving, but they lied to us. Later they told us that father had died. The funeral was very sad. Very few people came because the Germans did not permit it – they did not allow any gatherings. At home it was sad and difficult.

As typhus spread in the town, hunger became more severe because the farmers were afraid to come in to town where every door had a sign saying "Typhus." The delivery of food stopped almost entirely. At home it was difficult. My brother signed up to do hard manual labour for the Germans. He received three hundred zlotys every month as well as soup. The soup was shabby, but even that bit of warm soup stilled one's hunger. He also received an identity card. We lived by selling off our things. My father's suit and coat, as well as my mother's clothing. We did not have a lot saved because we always lived hand-to-mouth. My mother was very observant and she did not want to accept any help from our neighbours. She lived mostly on dry bread. She was even afraid to eat soup if she was not sure whether it would be kosher.[15]

My mother sent me to a farmer, Józef Rymniak [Rycuniak],[16] who lived in the village of Wolice about three kilometres from Komarów, and with whom she used to trade. Mother sent me to work as a shepherd. The farmer took me in. Mother warned me against eating meat

---

15 See page 175, note 7 and the glossary.

16 In 2007, Adam Shtibel confirmed that the name of the farmer he worked for in the summer of 1941 was Józef Rycuniak. With the exception of this passage, in which an error of transcription apparently occurred, he is correctly referred to as "Rycuniak" in the rest of the Polish-language document containing the transcription of Adam's 1948 testimony.

and lard, and told me to drink only milk and eat bread. Mother also gave me father's prayer book and told me to pray every day.

I left our house before noon. The cows were in the pasture [when I arrived]. Edek, the owner's son, minded them. They also had one Polish farmhand, Józek. He did all the work in the field. I only looked after the cows. The family consisted of the owner's wife, Marina, the owner himself, Józef, his son, Edek, who attended the village public school, and his daughter, Basia, who helped out with the housework. The [farm] work was left to Józek and me. Everybody treated me well and Józek was a good fellow. We both slept in the hay in the barn. We were good friends. I helped him mill the grain and, in return, he cut me big pieces of bread. The farmer's wife was very sly and would always cut small pieces of bread. I was timid and did not want to go near the bread, but Józek was daring; he would cut the bread himself and give me some.

I always kept the prayer book with me. One time, Józek and I were sleeping in the hay and I had covered myself with my jacket. I did not notice that the prayer book had slid from my pocket and fallen into the hay. Józek found it and asked what it was. I told him it was my prayer book. One time, Edek also found my little book and laughed at me. I could not say my prayers out in the field because I was always in the company of shepherd boys there and they would laugh at me. So I had to wait until Friday night, for *Shabbes*. Every *Shabbes*, I went home to my mother. The farmer's wife always gave me some food – potatoes, cabbage, some peas, bread and milk to take home. I brought all this to my mother. When I came home I went to pray in a *minyen* [prayer group] at the rabbi's house. My mother made *chullent* [a traditional stew]. The Germans had taken away our candlesticks, so mother had to put the [Sabbath] candles directly on the table. These *Shabbes* days were not like they used to be when father was alive. Then *Shabbes* was a holiday in the house. The table was covered with a white tablecloth and the house smelled clean. There was fish and cake and father said *kiddush* [the blessing on the wine]. Now,

Shabbes at home was poor and pitiful. By Sunday morning, I was already back at the farmer's house. On Sundays, Józek went over to his friends to have a good time, and I would lie in the hay and sleep.

It became more and more difficult to go home [to Komarów] for *Shabbes.* Returning to the village [afterward] was particularly difficult. There were a lot of Germans on the roads. People would run away when they saw Germans. I was afraid to do the trip because each time I paid with my health. In the village everyone said that things were going to get worse for the Jews.

One Friday, I came home for *Shabbes.* I was supposed to return to the village on Sunday, but early [Saturday] morning the Germans surrounded our town. I tried to escape to the farmer's house, but the Germans were hiding along the roads. There were a lot of Germans and I had to return home. A neighbour made a hiding place in our home. He lifted several floorboards, dug a hole and put the bed on top of it to hide the cracks in the floor. I wanted my mother to hide in there. There was not enough room for both of us in this hiding place, however, and my mother wanted me to hide in there. She was going to go to the square where Jews were being rounded up for deportation.[17] I did not want her to do that so I forced my mother into the hiding place and remained in the house along with my brother.

There was screaming and shouting in the street. The Germans walked from house to house chasing everybody out. They beat up everybody, children, old people, the sick – everybody. They came into our house. My brother showed them his identity card and was let go immediately. I, on the other hand, was kicked and driven out to the place where all the Jews were gathered. We were put into groups of four. There was shouting and wailing. The Germans walked around with rifles, nobody could get away. We were told to bring along our

---

17 The deportation of Jews from Komarów began on Saturday morning, May 23, 1942. *Pinkas Hakehillot Polin,* 468.

things as we were being resettled to another city. I saw a German hit a hunchbacked Jew who was probably not standing straight in his row. He clobbered him mercilessly on the head and in the face with a thick rubber hose until the invalid had no strength left to scream and groan. I had the shivers – it was the first time in my life that I saw a person being beaten so savagely and I was afraid.

I noticed a boy leaving the place where the Jews were gathered. When he was stopped by a German, the boy gestured that he was going to get a drink of water. So, I too turned to exit. A German stopped me and I told him I was going to get a drink of water. He ordered me to turn back, but I pretended not to hear him and walked on. I slipped away from the gathering place. The town was already empty. Nobody stopped me. I walked through the town. There were many dead people on the street. The Germans had killed those who tried to escape on the spot.

I left the town and lay down in a field. I watched as the Jews were taken away on carts. Each cart was supervised by a German. I waited in the field until dusk. Once it was dark, I went along side streets to our house. Silence reigned all around. One could hear every step and every movement. Now, the people who had been hiding in their houses and basements began to come out. I went into our home. My mother and our neighbour had left their hiding place and were already inside the house. They were happy to see me alive and were astonished by the miracle that had saved me. I spent the night at home. The next day mother told me to go back to the farmer in the village. The road through the town and beyond was quiet. I did not run into anybody. My employer did not know that I was alive. They received me very well. They were pleased that I had returned to work for them.

Only those who worked and had identity cards, or who had succeeded in hiding during the deportation action, now remained in the ghetto. The Jewish Council was still there.[18] There was sadness in our town. Every Jew lived in fear that at any moment the Germans would come and take him away. I still returned home from time to time, but not as often as before.

There was one Jewish policeman, Jamcie, who wanted to please the Germans by beating and torturing Jews. He was a buddy of the German policeman Ne. When new German police arrived [in Komarów], they killed that policeman [Jamcie].[19] At the time, I was in the village [Wolice], but people told me about it.

About two weeks after the first deportation, German military police arrived.[20] They took all the Jews, including the chairman of the Jewish Council, to the Jewish cemetery and killed them there. A few were left untouched. When I came home for *Shabbes*, I learned about all these events.

Jews who worked for the Germans and had identity cards and those who hid remained in the ghetto. After a while, just before Christmas [1942], and about two weeks or so after the liquidation of the [rest of the] Jewish Council, the Germans were back in town and deported the remaining Jews.[21]

I was in the village at the time. From early in the morning on, one could hear shooting coming from the direction of Komarów. People said that the rest of the Jews were being finished off. The operation

---

18 The Germans often delayed the deportation and murder of members of the Jewish Council until after the majority of the ghetto population had been removed.

19 Even though the Jewish police exercised considerable power within the ghetto, to the Germans these policemen were "just" Jews and subject to the same fate.

20 In early June 1942.

21 The Komarów ghetto was fully liquidated in November 1942. The remaining Jews were either shot in and around the town or deported and killed in nearby Belzec. Belzec was a death camp where more than 600,000 Jews and several thousand Gypsies were murdered between March and December 1942. *Pinkas Hakehillot Polin*, 468; Bergen, 178.

lasted all day. In the evening, the Jews were taken from Komarów to Zamość. From there, they were taken to an unknown destination by train.[22] One of our neighbours, Shmul, escaped from this hell. He ran away from the train and wandered across the roads and fields. I met him that same day and he told me what had happened in the ghetto. I asked him about my mother and brother, but he had not seen either of them. Not until the next day did the news reach us. We heard that the sick, the old and the children had been taken to the cemetery and shot dead. The rest of the Jews were deported. Village boys entered the homes of the deportees, looting them and looking for Jews that they could report to the Germans. When the Polish police caught Jews, they put them in jail in Komarów, a fortified place not far from the police station.

Things became worse for us. The day after [the liquidation of the Komarów ghetto], the *soltys* [chairman of the village council of Wolice] received an order that no Jews were allowed to remain in the village. All Jews had to be handed over to the police. The chairman called all the farmers to a meeting and informed them of the order. After the meeting, some of the farmers were afraid to keep Jews and did as the chairman said. In other cases, they told their [Jewish] farmhands to leave, but did not hand them over to the police.

The farmer's wife called me and said, "You know what, Abram, I met your mother and she told me that you should come home. I am going to give you bread and then you should go home to her." I told her that this was not true, that she had not been to the town. Then she told me the truth about the order not to shelter Jews and that I had to leave her house. My farmer came to me and told me that I was a good boy and that he would gladly keep me if the whole thing would be over in a few weeks. But keeping me permanently was out of the

---

22 When Adam gave his testimony in March 1948 he did not know that the deportees had been taken to Belzec.

question because the situation was getting worse – no Jew was to be allowed to live. He gave me some bread and told me to go wherever I wanted. He also told me that if I was in the vicinity and was sure that nobody saw me, I could drop in for some food.

I was in a bad situation. I did not know where to go or whom to ask for advice about what to do. I thought, "What will be, will be." I did not go in the direction of our town, but went through the fields that lay ahead of me. I did not take the roads, but walked through the fields and clearings. It became dark and I was still walking by myself. In one field there was a haystack. I was cold, freezing, so I crept into the haystack and fell asleep. I slept through the night. At dawn, I got up, stuffed myself with the bread I had and moved on.

I got to a small forest where I met a group of Jewish boys and girls from our town, Komarów. They, like me, had had to leave their farmers and were now walking around in the woods. I was somewhat relieved and in a better mood. I asked them about my mother and brother, but nobody knew anything. We told ourselves that cats and dogs had it better than we did: a cat has his oven, a dog his kennel, but we were being chased like rabbits from one place to another. For the time being, we stuck together. We were about eight or ten boys and two girls – all children. The oldest was perhaps seventeen years old, and the youngest, a girl, was maybe eight years old. We got along well with each other and shared our bread. Everyone was sad and we cried. I was worried because I did not know anything about my mother. I did not know if she had been caught or if she was in hiding. We slept on the leaves in the forest. I became friends with a boy, Yosel, whom I knew from the village. He had been herding cows not too far away from me. We stuck together, we slept and walked together.

One day we were sitting around a fire warming ourselves in the woods. We talked about the need to split into smaller groups because the [Polish] shepherd boys might notice us and give us away. We also decided that we should go ask for bread at the farmhouses. So we split up. I stayed together with Yosel. Yosel looked less Jewish than I did.

We spoke Yiddish amongst ourselves because we did not know Polish well.

It was already quite cold, with strong winds. It was too cold to sleep in the forest, so we snuck into the village barns and hid in the straw, where nobody would see us. We stayed in those barns for many days. In the evening we went out begging, sometimes together, sometimes separately, to collect more food. At first we did not know where a good farmer lived or a bad one. The worst ones were the farmhouses where there were children. They called us names, yelling, "Get out, scabby Jews, we will soon go to the Germans." They threw rocks at us and chased us. We did not go back to those farmhouses. We only tried the places where elderly people lived and where they would not chase us out. In some farmhouses, we were met with sympathy; they gave us dinner, hot soup, bread. They told us to eat fast and then get out. When people asked us where we were staying and sleeping, we always responded vaguely, "in the forest," not giving away any details.

We lived this way for about a week. We knew more or less how we would be received in some of the farmhouses. One day, we went into a barn and apparently the mistress of the house saw us. We buried ourselves in the straw and stayed there. After a long while we heard steps and voices in the barn. We thought that the farmer might be looking for something. The steps came closer and only then did I notice the policemen. Someone's feet stepped on me; they stopped, began shovelling away the hay and found us – Yosel and me. I came face to face with Polish policemen with rifles. The mistress of the house was standing in front of the door. The policemen yelled at us, "Get up and get out of here!" They chased us in front of them, hitting and hurrying us along. I began to cry and begged them to let us go, but they said they were taking us to the Komarów police station. They did not do anything to us, but they said, "This bullet," they pointed at the rifle, "will kill you." They pushed us with the rifle butts. We pleaded and begged them to let us go, but they joked and laughed at us. They were young policemen. We were already far away from the place where they had caught us. We continued crying and begged them to let us go, asking what they would gain by killing us. Yosel took out a purse in which he had some money (he had never told me about it or how much he had). He handed it over to one of the policemen. The policeman began counting the money and, before he had finished, told us to run away as fast as we could – like thunder! They stood watching us and we took off fast. As we ran away, we kept turning around to see whether they were following us. We saw that they had gone in a different direction. We made it to a small grove of alder trees where we rested for a while. We were relieved that the policemen had let us go because there were rumours that when they caught a Jew they didn't just shoot him, they tortured and murdered him in a terrible way. I was afraid of such torture and I was glad that Yosel and I were saved.

We agreed that we would stick together, that God had saved us together. We got along even better than before, like true brothers. We were very afraid. When the wind stirred the leaves, we thought that someone was coming to get us. But it was cold and wet in the forest and soon we again began to go from house to house begging for food. We avoided the barn where we had been caught, however. We had to calculate our comings and goings so as not to be noticed by the same households. We were always looking for new places to sleep. We kept an eye on one particular barn that was open most of the time, so it was easy to get in and hide. Most nights, we stayed there.

We were in poor shape – always hungry, dirty and unwashed. I had one shirt and it was covered in lice. My woollen sweater was also covered in lice and I had to throw it away. My shoes were in an even worse condition – they were falling apart.

But a worse misfortune was in store for me. One day Yosel and I were walking on the road and we met one of his friends with whom he had herded cows – they knew each other well. This boy was older than us. He had a light complexion, blue eyes and blond hair, did not look Jewish, and spoke Ukrainian well (because he had been working for a local Ukrainian farmer). Yosel was dark but did not look Jewish.

I was the one who looked the most Jewish of all of us. Right away they conspired to stick together and leave me behind. Yosel told me that we could not always stick together, that we had to separate. I begged him not to leave but to no avail. I did not want to leave them and remain alone. I cried, but my tears did not move them and they began to walk away. I asked them where they were going, but they did not want to tell me. I walked behind them, but they did not allow me to follow them. The boy hit me and they ran off. I could not catch up to them and remained behind alone.

Walking around alone, I became sad. I continued to beg for food and to sleep in the different barns that I came across. My situation worsened, nobody wanted to help me. I was dirty, covered in lice, hungry and without hope. I wandered alone through forests and fields.

I decided to return to my old employer Józef Rycuniak and decided to set out that afternoon. I walked straight on through forests and fields until I came to the village [Wolice]. The road was quiet. When I came close to the village, I noticed a man walking toward me. I turned back in the direction of the forest. The man sped up in order to follow me. I began to run and the man followed me. I could not run fast because my torn shoes made it difficult. I had to take them off and run barefoot. The man following me could not catch me and he returned to the village. I stretched out on the ground and decided to wait until the evening. My feet were frozen and in pain, but I could not stay there for long. I got up and slowly began walking back to the village in the darkness. The man was not there any more. He must have become bored waiting for me for so long. The village was quiet; people were probably sleeping. As I got closer to the village barns, about five people suddenly jumped on me shouting, "Stop! Stop!" I tried to get away quickly, but they were right behind me. My shoes were in such a state that they slowed me down even more [than before]. They caught me. One of them recognized me and said, "This is little Abram who worked for Rycuniak." These farmers were the village guards. I begged them to let me go. I was shaking all over, but they took me to [the home of] the *soltys* and told me to sit down.

The *soltys* was not at home at that time. His wife was quite polite to me. She asked where I had been and what I had been doing. I told her that I had nowhere [to stay], that I was wandering through fields and forests. In any case, my appearance made it plain that I was homeless and just roaming around. The *soltys* returned. They spoke amongst themselves, I did not know about what, but it seemed that they had decided to hand me over to the Germans. But the next day, they took me to an empty hut where nobody lived. They locked me up and left. As I was knocking about in the hut, it occurred to me that this would be the end of me. When it grew quiet in the village, I walked over to the window and noticed that it was low and not tightly closed. After a few hours, once the village was asleep, I opened the window hooks and quietly opened the shutters. I left the window open, quietly snuck out into the garden and crouched low in the grass. I moved around the barns very quietly until I got to my farmer's barn. There was no dog there and nobody was guarding it. The barn was closed but not locked. I crept into the hay and fell asleep immediately.

The next morning, the farmer came to get hay. I went over to him right away and told him everything, how I had escaped and what had happened to me. The farmer was pleased and said that I was a brave boy. He sent his wife to me with food right away. When she came, she brought bread, milk, potatoes and baked dumplings wrapped in a bag (it must have been a Sunday because I remember that we only ate dumplings on Sunday). I ate until I was full and then spent the whole day in the hay. After so many days of wandering and hunger, I finally had a sense of well-being. I did not want to think about anything. I wanted to take advantage of this moment of peace and quiet.

In the evening they brought me into the house to eat and to warm up. Everybody sat around me. The children encircled me and asked questions about where I had been and where I lived. I told them everything and they listened attentively. They pitied me, but unfortunately, they could not help me. The farmer told me that I had a good, warm winter coat and I would be able to survive the winter in it, but I had no shoes and that was bad. They gave me laces to tie up my shoes. I stayed with them for another two days. The farmer did not have the heart to tell me I had to leave. He sent his wife to tell me that she was afraid to have me stay any longer and that I should leave. They gave me food for the road, bread and some milk. They fed me soup and dumplings, everything they had in the house. I said goodbye. The farmer was sad. He wanted to help me, but he said he could not. He told me very clearly that if my situation became very bad, I could come again for a few days to warm up and to eat. I had to make sure that nobody from the village saw me. I was sad to say goodbye and in the evening I left.

Once again I was miserable; once again I did not know where to go. I walked almost all night. I was afraid. Every movement in the forest scared me. I was not afraid of ghosts, I was afraid of people. When a rabbit ran, I thought it was a man. I wanted to go to the barn where I used to spend the night, but as if out of spite I could not find it. I walked on. I came across another barn. I crept in, buried myself in the straw and stayed there the whole day. I could hear people walking, but I did not dare move. For the time being, I had food. The worst thing was that I was covered in mountains of lice. Lice wandered all over me and the straw in which I slept was covered with them. I had to be frugal with the food. I tried to eat as little as possible so it would last as long as possible. But in the end the food ran out and I had to leave. I left at dusk.

From a distance I noticed an old, little house. I always tried to seek out poor, elderly people. This was a house where such people lived. They gave me soup and bread. They asked me about my family. I told them the truth. They pitied me but could not help me. The villagers complained that things were hard for them as well – that they were also being deported.[23] Some did not even let me pass the threshold, they were afraid. Others gave me a little food, but forbade me to show up again.

One time I was walking around looking for a hiding place. It was getting late and dark. I found a storage cellar under a house. I snuck in and lay beneath a pile of wood. Suddenly a woman came in to get some wood. Somehow I must have moved and scared her. She began screaming loudly, dropped the wood and yelled at me. She chased me out and screamed, "You scabby Jew, get lost!" I barely escaped alive. I wandered all night. Finally, in the morning, I snuck into another barn.

Once again I was on the move, always a different house and a different barn. One evening, I crept into a barn. In the morning, when I wanted to get up, I heard shouting, talking and carts rattling. I heard voices and German being spoken. All day I listened to the screams and the rattle of carts. Only in the evening did things quiet down – then there was dead silence. I was afraid to move and would not have left the barn had I not been so hungry. My hunger was like torture to me and I had to get out. I went into different houses, but no one was around, not a living soul, not a horse or a cow. I then realized that all the inhabitants from the village had been expelled.[24]

---

23 In the spring of 1943, with the Jews nearly all gone, German plans for the Zamość district – where Adam was wandering and hiding – increasingly turned to the deportation and forced resettlement of ethnic Poles. These actions were part of far-reaching Nazi plans to "Germanize" Poland through large-scale population transfers. The aim was to clear out large areas in the western and central parts of the country by moving Poles and other Slavs to the east and to resettle ethnic Germans, known as *Volksdeutsche* into the newly empty areas. In this period, young Poles, especially males, were also targeted for conscription to do forced labour in Germany. Pohl, 95; Bergen, 107–108, 121.

24 In June and July 1943, the Germans intensified their campaign of forced transfer and resettlement of the ethnic Polish population in the Zamość district. The aim was to relocate 60,000 ethnic Germans into Zamość and its surrounding areas by

I walked from one empty house to another in search of food. In one house, I found bread and milk skins in the kitchen – I ate my fill. Dogs wandered around the houses and in the yards. I was standing near the stove eating when suddenly I heard steps and banging. I hid behind the stove. They found me. I saw five people in black clothing with rifles in front of me. They spoke German. They ordered me to get out.

They asked me what I was doing there while shining their flashlights in my face. I told them that my aunt lived here, that I had come from Wolice to see my aunt, but I could not find anybody. I did not know that I would not find anybody here. No one told me that I would not find anybody so I was looking for her. They asked me where I lived. I told them it was far away and that I had walked for a long time and was hungry. They spoke to me in German and I answered them in German. I did not even realize that I was speaking German to them so freely. They said that since my German was so good, I must be a Jew. I told them that I was Polish. They asked me again how come I knew German so well. They pushed me with their rifles and chased me ahead of them. I began crying – I thought they were going to shoot me.

They took me to the better houses [in the village], those occupied by Germans after the Poles were expelled.[25] They brought me

---

the end of 1943. Adam was caught up in the operation known as "Wehrwolf Aktion I and II," during which more than 100,000 Poles from nearly three hundred villages were expelled. This operation is viewed by many as the most violent deportation of non-Jews during the war. During the expulsions, many Poles were deported to the death camps at Auschwitz and Majdanek. Pohl, 95; Bergen, 107–109, 122–123; Jozef Garlinski, "The Polish Underground State, 1939–1945," *The Journal of Contemporary History*, 10 (1975): 229; Gotz Aly, *"Final Solution": Nazi Population Policy and the Murder of the European Jews*, trans. Belinda Cooper and Allison Brown (London and New York: Arnold, 1999).

25 As part of their effort to Germanize the Polish territories, German authorities

to a house where a German family lived. One of the men in black told them that they had found a boy who knew German very well. I explained to them that there were Germans living in my village. I cleaned their shoes and brought them water and this is why I spoke German so well. They believed me and gave me food. I ate my fill and then they let me go. I told them that I was going to go back home to Wolice.

I left and went to the forest not far from the houses. It was very cold. I walked around in the forest for the entire [next] day. At dusk, I approached the houses and went into one of the empty ones – the new inhabitants had not arrived yet. I ate some food that I found. I put the leftovers in a bag for the road. But, once again, the Germans came in, probably the same ones as before, because they recognized me immediately. Right away, they began yelling at me that I was a smart aleck – that I had lied to them, stolen food and that I was a crook. I did not say anything. I understood that this was the end of me. They told me to get out. I wanted to take my little bag but they yelled at me to leave everything. They ordered me to walk in front of them following me with their rifles. They chased me down quite a stretch of the road until we got to the village guardhouse. They told me to empty my pockets. I had some dried out tobacco and gave it to them, but they did not want it. They only wanted weapons. I told them that I did not have any. They searched me but did not find anything. One of them was ordered to take me to the cellar. I ran in front and he followed with a rifle. The cellar was dark. He pushed me into the cellar and locked the door with a key. I walked around and realized that there were other people in the cellar. I thought I heard someone speak Yiddish. I assumed that they were Jews so I replied in

---

"replaced" the deported Polish population with ethnic Germans who took over the empty farms and homes. While the expulsion and forced resettlement of Poles intensified in the spring and summer of 1943, it had been going on since late 1941.

Yiddish. I heard other voices. Someone asked me, "Are you Jewish?" I said, "Yes, I am." They asked me where I was from and how I had gotten caught. I told them everything. I asked them who they were. They were Poles. Poles who had been expelled from the village. They had run away [during the deportation], but had been caught and put in prison here.

When daylight came, I could see their faces. They were young village boys. We remained in this cellar for three days. The only thing we talked about was how we might get out of there. Since I was the smallest, they wanted me to get out through a small window and open the door to the cellar so that they could escape.

They discussed among themselves whether they should hand me over to the Germans because I was a Jew. One of them said they should not do it. I begged them not to say anything because, if the Germans had not recognized me [as a Jew] when they arrested me, they certainly would not recognize me now. I decided not to talk about it any more. During those three days in the cellar, nobody showed up, nobody gave us any food. After three days the door opened and the policemen in black appeared and told us to get out. They ordered us to climb onto a cart where there were three Germans to guard us. Then they took us to Zamość to a camp for Polish displaced persons.[26] The road was difficult. The Germans told the three boys to walk all the way, but since I was the smallest they left me on the cart. They dropped us off behind the barbed wire [surrounding] the camp where there were already a lot of people. We had to register in an office and everyone had to give their personal information. For some reason, the boys did not want me to stay with them. They wanted to

---

26 This camp for repatriated or displaced Poles was established in Zamość by the
Germans in late November 1942 and was used as a transit point to facilitate
the implementation of their population policies. It existed until January 1944.
Czeslaw Pilichowski, ed., *Obozy hitlerowskie na ziemiach polskich 1939–1945* (Warsaw: Panstwowe Wydawnictwo Naukowe, 1979), 583.

get rid of me, to mix in with other people. But I tried to stay with them. They kept avoiding me until I finally lost sight of them.[27]

I joined the crowd and went to line up for registration. I did not know what to say. Then I had an idea. As my name, I would state "Józef Rycuniak." I remembered [and used] the name of the farmer I had worked for in the village of Wolice in the rural commune of Sniatyce of Zamość district. I told them that I was twelve years old.[28] As my father's name I gave the name Stanislaw Jan Rycuniak, [who had been] a neighbour. They ordered me to go to one side. They immediately separated the youths from the older people and children. For every four children, they assigned an older person as a caretaker. My caretakers were an older couple and we were joined by two brothers and one girl, who were probably also orphans. The youths were sent to do labour in Prussia.

My caretakers were good people. I told them that I did not know how to say my prayers or how to cross myself, so they knew that I was Jewish. I told them that my parents had died when I was two years old so I did not have anybody who could teach me. My caretakers began giving me smaller portions of bread.

In general, people had their own troubles and I was left alone. Only one boy, an orphan, kept yelling at me that I was a Jew. But nobody had the time to pay any attention to me. The caretakers' only concern was that I had a clean shirt to put on and food. They did like me better than the other children because I was quiet, obedient and caused little trouble. The other children were mischievous. I did not

---

27 By the time Adam reached the displaced persons camp in Zamość, he had been wandering around the forests and villages of the district for approximately six months – that is, from the time he was told to leave Rycuniak's farm after the liquidation of the Komarów ghetto (late November 1942) to the time he was picked up and sent to Zamość following one of the expulsions of the Wehrwolf Aktion (June or July 1943).

28 In the summer of 1943, Adam was in fact fourteen years old.

play with the children because they were always making a mess. I was lonely.

My main preoccupation [at the camp in Zamość] was delousing myself. I worked a lot on my clothing. When I walked around begging for food, sometimes a stranger gave me a dry crust of bread. The barracks were dark, dirty and crowded with a lot of little children and older people. People were dying. Even though I was cold, I still preferred this to being in the forest. We stayed there for three weeks. My shoes were good for nothing. One elderly man was sick and we waited for him to die. He had a good pair of clogs and I wanted those clogs. But one girl wanted those clogs as well. People already suspected that I was Jewish, so when the old man died and this girl hurried over and pulled off his clogs, I remained without shoes again.[29]

---

29 Reviewing his testimony more than fifty years later, Adam recalled details of his experience in the camp in Zamość that he had not included in his 1948 testimony: "Once a day in the afternoon, hot soup was served. People would line up holding their dish in their hands. I had no dish. I looked around and noticed an empty bottle lying on the floor in the corner. I picked it up. Then, I wrapped a string around the middle of the glass bottle, soaked it with kerosene and lit it with a match. When the bottle was hot, I knocked off the neck with a piece of wood. I was happy because I now had a dish. I lined up for soup. When my turn came, the man serving the soup refused to fill my glass bottle. He said that some glass might fall into the big soup kettle, so I would have to come back after everyone else was served. When there were no people left in line, I returned and he gave me very thick soup from the bottom. Later the man called out, 'Who wants a repeat?' I jumped up and went over to him. He filled my bottle with thick soup again. Even though I was still hungry, I did not finish it as I wanted to save it for breakfast the next day.

"I slept near the door of the barracks. The walls shook from the constant slamming of the door by people going back and forth to the outhouse. While I was sleeping on my back, the bottle with the soup, which I had left resting on the narrow windowsill above my head, gradually moved until it fell on my face. A piercing pain woke me: my nose had been cut in half. My face was covered with blood and people around me screamed, 'Oh my God!' They felt sorry for me and

After three weeks, we, all the older people and children, were taken away [by train] to Siedlce.[30] They took us at night and we arrived there in the morning. One boy who tried to escape from the train was shot dead by the Germans. The Germans guarded us strictly the whole time.

They brought us to the Red Cross in Siedlce.[31] Soon, many people from the city came with food and old clothing. They asked us where we were from and wanted to take care of us. Older people with acquaintances or relatives went with them to church. The Germans returned [to Zamość] and we were free to move around in the city of Siedlce. Small children were immediately placed in private homes, but I had nowhere to go. I had terribly long black hair. I was afraid that people might recognize me [as a Jew]. I asked several boys my age to come with me to a barber in the city because I did not know the way. One woman gave me some money and I promised to pay them if they took me. As soon as we entered the [barber] shop, the barber began to shout that we were Jews and that we should leave right away. He refused to cut my hair. We left and five urchins, little boys, immediately surrounded us and began to chase us yelling loudly, "Jews! Jews!" They picked on one of my friends calling him "Icek" and said they knew him.[32] They picked on me less, but I was afraid. I asked

---

urged me to go to see the camp doctor. Being Jewish, I knew that I could not show my face to a doctor working with the Nazis. Instead, I tried to clean up my face. Part of my nose was hanging off and I tried to support it by tying a string around my nose and head. My nose did not heal very well, because I did not take any medication or receive any treatment. I suffered for a very long time."

30 Siedlce is a small city north of Lublin and east of Warsaw, approximately two hundred kilometres from Zamość.

31 The Red Cross was one of the few Polish institutions allowed by the Germans to continue working in occupied Poland. The Red Cross assisted the repatriation and resettlement of displaced Poles into areas approved by the Germans. Pohl, 102.

32 "Icek" is a diminutive form of the name "Yitzhak" and was easily recognizable as a Jewish name.

them to follow us and see for themselves where we were going.[33] I was frightened the whole way, because the urchins did not stop yelling "Jews! Jews!" loudly. There were Germans all around us and we could have gotten caught. When we reached the gate of the Red Cross, the urchins took off and left us alone.

I did not go into the city again. I was quiet and did not want to spend time with the boys anymore. At least I was not hungry anymore. A woman gave me gloves and shoes and I felt better. People came to the Red Cross to choose children, but no one wanted to take me – they said I was a Gypsy.[34]

A young woman approached me and asked me whether I would like to come with her. I agreed. It was already after seven o'clock in the evening and the [German] guards did not want to let us through. The young woman spoke German well and convinced the Germans to let us through. She took me to a nice house, where they gave me a thin slice of bread, a thick piece of lard and a knife. I did not know how to eat it so I sliced the bread and took a bite of the lard. They looked at me with surprise. I remember that I felt confused and unhappy even though the food was good. I would have preferred no food at all to being looked at in this way. For the first time in a long while, I got to look at myself in the mirror. My appearance scared me. I was very dirty and I had a lot of hair.

The young woman took me to the railway station. We were going to go to her house near Warsaw. As we were standing in the Siedlce station, the young woman was approached by an acquaintance. She told him that she had taken me from the Red Cross to work [for her]. The man looked at me, observing me closely for a time. Then the

---

33 As no Jews were sheltered by the Red Cross, the fact that the boys were living there offered "proof" that they were not Jewish.

34 Being labelled a Gypsy was potentially as lethal as being found out as a Jew: Gypsies under German occupation were being ghettoized and killed alongside Jews. Bergen, 180.

man and the woman went aside to talk. She told me to wait there for her and that she would return shortly. I stood waiting for an hour, two hours, but the woman did not show up. I was cold and sleepy, so I went into the waiting room where many people were sitting and sleeping. I lay down on the floor, curled up and fell asleep. I slept until the morning.

When I woke up, everybody got on the trains. I was the only one that did not know where to go or what direction to take to leave the station. I just stood there. A cabman walked over to me and asked, "What are you doing here, little boy?"[35] I told him everything: that a young woman had picked me up at the Red Cross, that I had lost her at the train station and that now I did not know where to go. The cabman told me to get into his carriage. He dropped me off not far from the Red Cross and showed me how to get there. The guards did not want to let me in. After I explained everything that had happened to me, they let me in. I felt as if I was in heaven. I went to see my caretaker and told him everything. He gave me food and I calmed down.

A few days later, a farmer came. My caretaker praised me a lot. The farmer took me to a physician to have my health checked. I was infested with lice and the physician was afraid to touch me. I was barely undressed, but the physician did not even want to look at me. He said I was healthy and he let me go. The lice saved me. Since the physician had not examined me thoroughly, he did not discover that I was a Jew.[36] The farmer took me out into the street and quietly said, "Listen, you are a Jew, admit it. If you are not Jewish, come to a German doctor." He argued with me and added, "If you are a Jew, it would be better not to take you to a German doctor." I said firmly, "If

---

35 A cabman was a driver of a horse-drawn carriage available for hire and to make deliveries.

36 According to Jewish religious practice, Jewish boys are circumcised soon after birth. As this was not the practice of non-Jews in Poland, a physical examination would have disclosed that Adam was Jewish.

you want, you can take me; if not, somebody else will. I am not Jewish." He went away and left me behind. I returned to the Red Cross. I was embarrassed to face my caretaker again, but I somehow got over it (I do not remember what I told him).

Fewer and fewer children remained in the Red Cross. People had picked them up. Only the sickly and helpless children were left and I was among them.

After a few days, the cabman [from the Siedlce train station] and his wife came to the Red Cross. They approached me and asked whether I wanted to come with them. Once again, my caretaker praised me saying what a good boy I was. They told me to take everything I owned and they took me with them. His carriage was in the marketplace. They told me to get in and they took me to their house not far from Siedlce. It was a plain house. They had a horse, piglets, a meadow and a garden – and nothing else. They allowed me to wash and gave me a clean shirt and trousers. They dressed me in clean clothes. They boiled all my clothes and took my coat to the barn so it could air out. They told me that I was going to be a shepherd.

They questioned me about everything. I told them that my parents had passed away when I was three years old and that I had been brought up by my uncle in a village, that when the Poles were expelled, they had taken my uncle to Prussia, and that his children had [already] been taken from the Red Cross – and so on. In the evening, the neighbours came over with their children, boys, and they asked me questions. I had to lie again and again. It was difficult because I had to find an answer on the spot and I had to remember what I had said earlier – often I did not. This tired me out.

They asked me to say a prayer before I went to sleep and I did not know how to cross myself. I said, "My uncle did not care about it and that is why I do not know." They believed me and the mistress of the house taught me how to cross myself and how to pray. Little by little, I learned. Later, I played with the neighbours' children. The kids liked me and did not want to go anywhere without me. The people were nice to me. They gave me better food. The lady of the house even gave me cracklings [fried pork rinds] that she saved for me. She treated me like her own child. But I overheard the neighbours who visited claim that I was a Jew over and over again. After a week, they began mumbling more and more often that I was a Jew. My guardians also began to look at me differently. They began questioning me, but I did not admit it.

One day, when the cabman was not home – he had gone to the city – his wife came over to me, examined me and discovered that I was Jewish. She laughed, "So you are a little Jew!" I told her that I had been converted. But she did not believe me. When the man came home, his wife told him that she had discovered that I was a Jew. They spoke to me in a friendly way. They told me that once the war was over, I could come back to them, I could open a store and they would convert me. As I had said that I had already been converted, the man wanted to keep me, but his wife did not – she was afraid of the neighbours. The next morning, she fed me well. She did not take back the things that she had given me. I packed the clothes that had been boiled. She wrapped my coat with the lice in paper and went with me to the Red Cross. She declared that she was returning me.

Once again, I was left behind. Luckily for me, I had been absent when they disinfected the place and bathed the people. I had missed this because I was at the cabman's house. Many changes had taken place at the Red Cross. There were fewer people and the place was cleaner. I left the parcel with my coat in the hall. I did not want to take it with me. My caretakers [from Zamość] were no longer there.

After a few days, they announced that people who wanted to go to a village [to work] could do so. The Red Cross would provide carts and place people in different villages. Together with a family that had a little girl, I was assigned to the village of Borki.[37] We had to change

---

37 Borki is a small village located approximately thirty-five kilometres to the south-west of Siedlce.

carts in each community we passed. They took us to the village of
Borki. The *soltys* [chairman of the village council of Borki] assigned
homes to the displaced persons. The family I had come with received
a house for themselves. The *soltys* said to his wife, "Such a good-looking dark boy; if nobody wants to take him, he will remain with us." I
spent the night at the *soltys*' house, where they fed me.

The next day, the *soltys* gave me a card and sent me with a messen-
ger boy to the farmer Janek Szelag.[38] The farmer was at the mill and

----

38 Adam later recalled an important episode that he had not included in his 1948
testimony. Prior to going to work for Janek Szelag, he worked for another farmer:
"After arriving in Borki, the *soltys* gave me a slip of paper and had his boy take me
to a farmer called Józef Maciejak. When I arrived, I was met by a small family,
a husband, his wife and two small children. The farmer explained that I would
work as a shepherd. All he owned was one cow and a very small field. He in-
structed me to graze the cow on the neighbour's pasture, which I did. One time,
it was a rainy day, I was quite sure that nobody would come by, so I took the cow
over to the neighbour's pasture. Suddenly, a farmer came galloping over on his
horse. Using his whip he beat me all over my body and on my head while screaming at me, 'If I catch you on my pasture again, I will break your neck.' I took off
with the cow and went back to the cowshed. I told Maciejak what had happened,
but he just told me, 'Well, next time take the cow over to the other neighbour's
pasture.' He was very mean and did not feel sorry for me at all. Even though I was
soaking wet from the rain and hurt from the whipping, he told me to chop wood
outside in the rain.

"Józef Maciejak was a frequent visitor at the village tavern and he often came
home drunk. His wife was a very nice woman. She would make him a good sup-
per, but sometimes he would look at the set table, throw everything on the floor
and yell at her, 'What kind of dog food did you make?' Then he would corner
her and begin punching her in the face. She cried and screamed. Her two little
children and I would jump up and crawl under the bed, afraid that we might
be next. These episodes were very frequent. I was not allowed to take any bread
without first asking permission. I was made to eat by myself, rather than with the
family, and I slept alone in the barn. Although I was treated poorly, I was happier
than I had been in the camp in Zamość and in the forest. The farmer used me
during the summer of 1943 but soon sent me back to the *soltys*. I was consumed

his wife told me to wait. The farmer came back covered in flour. He thought and then said, "One can tell that he is polite. If he stays here, he can herd the cows." They told me to stay. They were young people, but they did not have any children. The farmer's wife was unwell and often stayed in bed.

The next day, a village boy brought me a note from the chairman to report to him for registration. I did not know the way [back to the village]. My farmer told me to take a horse. I did not know how to ride a horse. I fell off the horse several times, but I got there somehow. One neighbour, Wozniak, recognized me and asked me where I was going. I could not remember how to say the word *soltys*. So I answered him, "The place I was at yesterday." He said, "That's here, the *soltys'* place."

I went inside and saw two [Polish] policemen sitting there. They asked me what my name was. When I told them that I came from the *gmina Sniatyce* [the rural commune of Sniatyce], I mispronounced the word *gmina*. My pronunciation gave away that I was a Jew. They began teasing me, asking me whether I knew how to pray. I said that I prayed every morning and evening. They teased me saying that I prayed from morning to evening. They ridiculed me and told me to cross myself and to say the prayers. I remembered the time when the cabman's wife taught me how to pray and I began reciting. They interrupted me. One of the policemen tapped me on the shoulder and said that I was a Jew. I argued with him. The *soltys* declared that I had come officially from Siedlce and that I was most certainly a Pole. He registered me and told me to go back to my farmer. I could not find

---

with worry about whether anyone would take me in. When I arrived at the *soltys'* house, I told him everything that had happened to me. He said, 'I will send you to another farmer and if he does not take you in then I will keep you with our family.' I stayed overnight and the next day he sent me to a farmer called Janek Szelag."

my way back and just let the horse guide me. I told my farmer that I had been registered.

I did not have much to do. I paced around the farmhouse. From to time to time, the farmer told me to put straw under the cows, to feed the horse and to bring some wood. I had to answer questions from the neighbours constantly. This tired me out because I had to answer quickly without thinking for too long and to remember all the little details that I had mentioned yesterday or the day before. Another difficulty was the food. I was a bit ashamed that I did not know how to eat the way they did in the village.

Everybody ate from the same bowl. The farmer told me to eat fast. I did not know how, but I picked it up little by little. I was not a good worker. I could only do the easiest jobs, but without work I would have gone completely crazy.

People often said I looked like a Jew. I denied this. When neighbours came to the house they often immediately recognized that I was Jewish and they would quietly tell my farmers about it. But my farmers always tried to protect me from having to answer questions. They spoke on my behalf and explained things about me, which helped me a lot. When nobody was around, they drew my attention to my pronunciation and corrected my mistakes. They made an effort not to send me to stores or to neighbours. I stayed at home most of the time. I did not even go to church. My farmers wanted me to go with them, but I found excuses by saying that I did not have suitable clothes or any shoes and that I would prefer to stay in the house. They did not insist that I go to church. And so it went.

The woman from Siedlce, whom my farmer met by accident, did me a lot of harm. Apparently, she told my farmer that I was Jewish. She told him what had happened to me in Siedlce and how farmers had taken me from the Red Cross several times, only to bring me back. My farmer told me that he knew about everything, but he did not do so openly. He was very good to me.

Since I was somewhat timid and shy, I did not dare cut bread for myself. The farmer told me that I should cut bread for myself as he did not begrudge me the bread, but that he could not know when I was hungry and wanted to eat. Gradually, I became less timid and began cutting bread for myself. Of course, I did not know how to do it and cut my hand instead of the bread. People laughed at me because I was so clumsy – [they said] "he has a cut on his hand."

One morning, when, as usual, I wanted to cut myself a piece of bread, the farmer's wife said, "We Poles do not eat today. Today is the day before the holiday, so today we fast."[39] I looked at her in surprise and asked what that meant. She explained it to me. I said, "I will not eat." I began putting away the milk and the bread. The farmer's wife said, "Eat since you already started." So I had to finish. Later, when Easter arrived, I did not know anything about it, how one behaved and what one was supposed to do. The farmers cleaned the house thoroughly. They prepared a lot of food. I felt like a stranger and did not know what to do. They cut my hair and told me to wash. They gave me a new shirt and new pants. All these customs were strange to me, but my farmers were good to me and did not laugh at my ignorance. They taught me and pointed out my mistakes. [On Easter,] they did not wake me up early in the morning. My farmer harnessed the horses himself and they drove off to church. They left me pancakes and cake and told me to eat. I got up and went to the farmer's parents to water the cows. Later, when they returned from church, it was time for the midday meal. It was good to eat something.

Neighbours frequently came by for a visit and they always asked me too many questions. The farmer's wife would then send me out to bring wood or water so that I would hear as little as possible of the neighbours' talk. I was happy that I had come across such good

---

39 Janek Szelag and his wife were Catholics and observed the first day of Lent, Ash Wednesday, by fasting. This incident occurred on February 23, 1944, about six months after Adam had gone to work for them.

people and was no longer wandering through forests and dirt, hungry and cold.

One time, the farmer's wife sent me to the village store to buy kerosene and matches. The store was in an inn crowded with people. As soon as I walked in, they all stared at me, saying quietly that I was Jewish. Then, when I asked for two packages of matches, I made a grammatical mistake and the store owner corrected me. Everybody laughed and said I was a Jew. I could have died of shame the way they spoke about Jews. I would always blush, which betrayed me, but I could not keep myself from blushing.

Whenever the Germans came for their quota of food, the farmer told me to drive out the cows so that I would not be in the house.[40] Once, I got a big scare: As I was driving out the cows, I suddenly saw Germans in front of me. What to do? I pulled my hat down over my eyes and pretended that I was chasing a cow from the side. I avoided the Germans.

I herded cows with other shepherds who became my friends. They asked me to come to the village one Sunday. Since I was lonely on Sundays, I decided to go. This was stupid. On the way to the village, there were groups of boys and grownups chatting. When they saw me, they began teasing me, "Mojsze wi goistu?" [in broken Yiddish, "Moshe, where are you going?"] I did not say anything pretending that it did not concern me. But I did not go to see my friends. I went home immediately through the barns rather than along the road.

As time passed, things got worse. People talked and spread rumours that I was Jewish, that I did not go to church, communion or confession, and that I looked like a Jew. There were always rumours going around that the Germans were looking for weapons and partisans, that they were catching Jews, that they had caught a group of

40 Farmers were required to supply the German authorities with goods and produce, facing imprisonment or worse if they did not do so. Pohl, 97.

children who used to beg out of the forest and other more terrible stories. The whole village put pressure on my farmers to get rid of me, saying that because they were sheltering a Jew, the whole village would suffer. These rumours spread to the neighbouring villages. Not far from us was the village of Strachanin [Strachomin].⁴¹ Everyone there talked about how Szelag kept a Jew. My farmer did not admit it. He never showed me that he knew about it. He always told me to hide in the rye field when the Germans came to the village so that they would not grab me to do forced labour.⁴² Later, my farmer made an effort to keep me at home.

When [my first] autumn arrived, I had been concerned that the work herding cows was coming to an end. If my farmer chased me out, what was I going to do? Where would I go? My farmer noticed how upset I was and asked me if I had a bellyache. I told him that I was always like that. But he understood and asked me if I wanted to stay the winter so that I could start herding cows again in the spring. I accepted with joy and said as much. They had gotten used to me and liked me.

Partisans would often come by. Once, when I was sleeping in the barn, the door opened and the farmer came in with a group of people. The farmer told me to help the partisans find a place to sleep. He had a flashlight and showed them the hay. The next day, one of the partisans said to my farmer, "You know, this Józef of yours moves like a Jew, he is most certainly a Jew." My farmer told him that I came from [the camp at] Zamość and that I was a displaced person. In the evening, the partisans got up and left.⁴³

41 An error of transcription apparently occurred during Adam's 1948 deposition. The name of the neighbouring village was Strachomin.

42 Young, able-bodied Poles were targeted for forced labour in Germany and in German industries throughout 1943 and 1944. Pohl, 93.

43 Partisans, members of Polish resistance groups, depended on the cooperation of farmers for food and shelter. There were several Polish resistance movements,

My farmer made moonshine. Whenever guests came over, he would invite me to the table and I would eat and drink with the guests. Once, I had to drive with a neighbour and he got me drunk. I was so drunk that I did not know what was happening to me. Apparently, I talked nonsense – swearing at my farmer because he said I was a Jew. I developed a taste for vodka and liked to drink, but I regretted that I talked like that.

Many things happened. One morning, the Germans arrived at the house of the *soltys* and together they went around to the homes of people who were to be drafted to do labour in Prussia. There was a big commotion in the village and the young people went into hiding. My farmer told me to hide in the cornfield. I remember that I was wearing new linen pants at the time. I did not want to damage them, but I had no choice but to lie down on the hard ground and wait for the Germans to leave the village.

The new *soltys*, Bronek Wysocki, was a wily man who manipulated people to the Germans' advantage. The Germans had demanded that ten boys from our village be sent to work in Prussia. The farmers held a meeting. One boy, Bronek, protested the choice of the boys being sent to work in Prussia. He demanded that my farmer send me to work there [instead]. He claimed that the other boys were needed for work in the village. They had a lot to do, while I was not doing anything and was therefore free to go work in Prussia.

Later, the son of one of the farmers was selected for work in Prussia and the *soltys* took a big bribe from the farmer to put me on the list instead. I received the notice but I did not report to the authorities. My farmer made me new clothes and told me that if people asked, I should tell them that I was going [to work in Prussia]. Then, when it came time to report for registration, my farmer took me to a farmer

---

often fiercely opposed to one another on ideological grounds, and at least one, the National Armed Forces, was violently antisemitic. Pohl, 104.

in another village and told everyone that I had run away. The next morning, I went to the pasture with the children and stayed there until the evening. In the evening I returned to the house and this was how time passed. Later on, I stayed overnight in the homes of other people that my farmer knew. My farmer's parents protested, saying that they would not let me go to Prussia and that they would not give me up to anybody. Once things quieted down and nobody was looking for me anymore, I returned home [to Borki].

I learned later that the partisans that used to come by my farmer's house kept an eye on me and wanted to get rid of me. I heard it from a neighbour, Kózicka. It was only thanks to my farmer that they left me alone.

People began talking about how the Russians were coming.[44] They had already occupied some villages and the Germans were retreating. One trader who came by my farmer's house kept saying that when the Russians came the Jews would be the rulers – he said it for my ears. At this time, even the Poles were afraid to leave their farms because they were afraid of the Germans. They said that the Germans were burning villages before leaving. It was a bad time for everybody. People said that the Russians were already in Siedlce. I hoped that I would live to see the Russians.[45]

The next morning, people said that the Russians were already in the village [of Borki]. My farmer and I went to see what the Russians looked like. On the road, we encountered trucks full of Russian soldiers. Right away the conversations were happy. The Russians were greeted with "Good health, comrades!" and were treated to cigarettes and candy.

---

44 In the summer of 1944.
45 The Red Army captured Siedlce on July 31, 1944.

Suddenly, German airplanes appeared. In Starachomine [Strachomin][46] shooting broke out and the Germans killed a horse and lit a few buildings on fire. Later, Russian planes appeared. The Russian soldiers [on the ground] told us that they were their planes and people calmed down and started celebrating with the Russians. The Russians were placed in the farmers' homes and people received them with pleasure and happiness.[47]

One evening, some Russian officers came by to visit. They asked me whether I was the farmer's son. One major immediately claimed that I was a Jew. My farmer said that I was not, and that I was a displaced person. The village boys would hang out with the Russians, but I remained by myself not knowing what to do and still afraid to say that I was a Jew.

A Russian major lived at our house. One time, he invited a guest, a Russian major from another village, who was a Jew. He recognized immediately that I was Jewish. My farmers told them that I was not. One village carpenter, Zbig, told me that I should admit that I was a Jew, but I would not do it. I decided to leave things as they were because I had heard that there were no more Jews in the world.

Later on, people tried to convince my farmers to convert me. His wife gave me a small book so that I could learn the prayers well and they coaxed me to convert. I did not say anything. They understood

---

46 See footnote 41

47 Borki was located in the area along and then just behind the front lines of the Soviet offensive that took place during the summer and fall of 1944, known as the Lublin-Brest offensive. This was the Red Army's major offensive to liberate central and eastern Poland and Warsaw. During the second half of 1944, Borki and neighbouring towns and villages became home to many Soviet soldiers and officers. David Glantz, "The Red Army's Lublin-Brest offensive and advance on Warsaw (18 July–30 September 1944): An overview and documentary survey," *The Journal of Slavic Military Studies*, vol. 19, no. 2 (June 2006): 401–441.

that I did not want to do it and they left me alone. Everything remained the same.

I had thought to myself that I would go to work in a factory in a city once the war was over. But for the time being, things remained as they had been. I decided to remain there and wait. Some of the villagers tried to convince me to leave my farmer and go work for them instead. [At my farm], I was working for nothing and [they said] that I would be better off working for them. But I knew what they had in mind and told them that I was satisfied at my farmer's and that I did not intend to leave him. I went on working. I was now very busy with my work, the horse, the fields, the hay, and time passed quickly.[48]

When I first moved in with my farmer, I became attached to a little horse who filled my time and gave me a lot of joy. He was my friend – a most beloved creature. I called him Siwek [the Grey One]. He, in turn, loved me and would only come to me. I saved the best bread and food for Siwek. He was the fastest runner in the village. He jumped over ditches and through fields. I trained him to come first in the races. I was so attached to Siwek that when one of the landowners [in the area] came to buy Siwek and my farmer wanted to sell him, I got very upset and begged my farmer not to sell him. One night, I dreamt that Siwek was breathing heavily and was sick. When I woke up, I did not go into the house to wash but instead went straight to the stable to see Siwek. I was happy to see that he was healthy. Another time, the estate manager wanted to buy Siwek. I cried and said

---

48 Adam remained with Janek Szelag and his wife in Borki for more than two years following the end of the war, never admitting that he was Jewish. In 2007, he recalled the thoughts and assumptions that kept him there: "I thought I was the only Jew who had survived. I still did not feel safe. I had no place to go. Everyone I had known from before was dead. I was certain that it was still not safe for me to admit that I was Jewish. After the war, the situation was still uncertain and tense – where would all the displaced people go? I felt it would be better to stay put, with people who had been good to me, rather than to take any chances."

that there would be no point in me going to the stable anymore and no reason for me to stay here. The farmer did not sell Siwek and I was overjoyed to have my beloved friend.

Whenever somebody suggested that I was Jewish, I would get angry and bad-tempered. My farmer noticed this and thought that I did not want to leave the village and return to be with Jews so he did not mention it again. Then our neighbour told me, "You know what, Józef, there are no more Jews anywhere. You have become used to the horses and the fields, stay with us, we will convert you and you will be with us. Nobody will touch you and you will be happy here." I did not say anything, but I thought that I would have to do it. Still, I had second thoughts and decided not to do it.

My best friend was a village boy, Kostek Walentow. We herded cows together in the forest. He went to visit his sister in the western part of the country [after the war ended]. When he returned, I went to talk with him. I asked him about the situation on the trains and whether they checked documents. What was the work situation like in the west? He was curious about why I was asking about all those things. Did I intend to go somewhere?

I told him that I would like to go to Warsaw. People kept telling me that I should go work in a factory in the west, like other boys.[49] I asked my friend how I could obtain documents. He told me to convert and get a birth certificate then I would be able to go anywhere. I stayed with him late into the night and told him everything. I admitted that I was Jewish, but asked him not to tell anybody.

A week later, he received a letter from his sister asking him to come west. Later, he wrote to his family [in Borki] that he got a job in the west and would not be coming back. I mentioned to my farm-

---

49 At the end of World War II, the German population living in the western part of Poland fled or was expelled. Work opportunities were thus created for Poles from the country's eastern regions. Bergen, 224–225.

er's wife that if someone as simple as Kostek and Ganiek could find
work in the west and decide not to return, then I could do the same
if I had documents. The farmer's wife asked me if I knew anyone in
the west. When I answered that I did not know anybody there, she
told me that going blindly was not worthwhile. She told me that my
farmer would go to see the *wójt* [the head of the rural commune] and
arrange documents for me. When the farmer came home, we talked
about it. He told me to wait until Sunday when he would see the *wójt*
in church. Then he would talk to him and something would be arranged. He kept his promise. My farmer asked the *wójt* for advice on
how to obtain a birth certificate. My farmer pointed out [to him] that
obtaining a birth certificate would be difficult because I was displaced
from Zamość and it was possible I was Jewish. Where could one obtain birth certificates for Jews now? The *wójt* said that he would find
out and let us know.

Around the same time, my farmer went to the fair at Latowicze
and he heard there that Jews could reclaim their houses, but only until the first of January [1948] (this was in 1947). My farmer led me into
another room and told me about it, asking me if I had a house left to
me by my parents or uncles. I told him that I did. We spoke for a long
time and for the first time I admitted to him that I was Jewish.

My heart jumped with joy now that it seemed that I would meet
Jews and could be myself again. We decided that my farmers would
go with me to Warsaw. They prepared me for the road, making me a
new coat and a new sweater.[50]

----

50 Adam later recalled how he finally came to understand that there were Jews still
  alive and Jewish organizations in existence and how he decided to go to Warsaw: "In the autumn of 1947, two traders came to the farm to buy a pig. I helped
  them catch the pig and tie him up. After we had put the pig on to their wagon,
  we went into the house. The farmer put a bottle of vodka and some bread and
  lard on the table to celebrate the deal. My farmer told me to sit down and have a
  drink, which I did. The men began asking me questions and said, 'You look very

One Sunday in the middle of December 1947, my farmer harnessed the horse and took us to Mrozów where we stayed with friends overnight. He told them we were going to Zamość for a birth certificate. I was so excited that I could not sleep all night. In the morning, [after Zamość,] we went by train to Warsaw. In Warsaw, my farmer's wife asked where the [Central] Jewish Committee was and we went there.[51] I was very excited and amazed that people spoke "German." I had completely forgotten Yiddish and thought they were speaking German. They received us very nicely and gave us tea.[52]

Jewish. Are you Jewish?' I was afraid to admit it so I answered, 'I am not Jewish.' They were not convinced by my answer and turned to my farmer saying, 'If he is Jewish then you can get a lot of money for him from the Central Jewish Committee in Warsaw,' and they left the address. This was the first time I had heard of the Committee, or of any Jewish organization, since before the war. I still wasn't certain it was true, but now that I understood that there were Jews alive, I was willing to say I was Jewish and try to get to Warsaw."

51 The Central Committee of Polish Jews was established in 1944 and was officially recognized as the highest administrative body of Polish Jewry. The Central Committee sought to reconstruct Jewish life in Poland. It received funds from the Polish government, as well as from the American Jewish Joint Distribution Committee, with which it financed its work caring for the remaining Jews of Poland. David Engel, "The reconstruction of Jewish communal institutions in postwar Poland: The origins of the Central Committee of Polish Jews, 1944, 1950," *East European Politics and Societies*, vol. 10, no. 1 (1996): 87–88.

52 Adam later recalled some of the details of this first post-war encounter with other Jews at the office of the Central Committee: "As we approached the door, we noticed a guard with a long beard leaving the washroom. At that moment, I was convinced that he was a Jew. I was thrilled because I was still not convinced that I was not the only Jew who had survived. He told me where to go in order to find the director, but I only trusted him and would not move on without him. He had no choice but to take us directly to the room. When he wanted to leave, I did not let him. As the director did not have a beard, I did not trust him. In my hometown all the Jewish men had beards, including my father. The director then explained to me that the whole building was full of Jews and that I would no

The people [from the Central Committee] took an interest in me and decided that I should go right away to a Children's House, called Zatrzebia. I was very confused. I did not know what to do with myself. I did not think about anything. I did what they told me. It was the first time in my life that I saw a big city. When I got on to a tram, I was surprised that so many people could travel in it and I was afraid that I was going to fall out. I completely forgot about my little horse. The farmer's wife convinced me to stay and to write to her. She promised that she would come and visit me. I listened to her.

In the beginning, I was amazed that I was not afraid to say openly that I was Jewish. It seemed to me that I was in a whole new world. Slowly I was introduced to a new life and various things were explained to me. I learned that there were still some Jews left, that many had returned from Russia and that some had survived here. I am not completely alone. Unfortunately, I did not find anybody from my family.

After a while, our [Children's] House moved to Warsaw to Jagielonska Street, to the student dormitory where I now live. I attend a school for young people and adults and I study Grade 4 and 5 material. A new world has opened up for me. I have learned many things that until now were completely hidden and unknown to me.

I do not want to return to the village, but I am very attached to my farmers and would like to help them as much as I can. I consider them my parents because they saved my life at the worst time. Now I write to them and I would like to go and visit them during the holidays. They write me warm letters saying they are lonely without me.[53]

---

longer have to be afraid. He told me that Jews were free now.

"My farmer's wife received some money. She did not get very much, because it had already been two and a half years since the end of the war and the director said that their funds had almost run out."

53 Adam did stay in touch with Janek Szelag and his wife for many years. They attended Adam's wedding to Rachel Milbauer in Wrocław in 1956. See Rachel

I would like to attend a trade school and learn a trade. I would like to be a mechanic and go to Palestine. There are many Jews there and I would not have to be afraid to be a Jew.

My whole life has been filled with pain and fear. When I recall the details, one seems scarier than the next. My most horrible experience was the deportation of the Jews from Komarów when I was separated from my mother, when I ran away from the gathering place that was full of Germans and when I was hiding alone in the field expecting death at any moment.

I have had terrible dreams several times. I always dream that the Germans have arrived, that they have caught me and that they are chasing me and killing me. One time, I dreamt that my brother perished, but that my mother was alive.

Now I think about the past all the time. My life is sad because I have lost my entire family. In the student hostel, I am the unhappiest one. Every child has somebody, one has an uncle, another an aunt, so that if he has no parents at least he has relatives. I do not have any relatives. I don't even have a relative I can get a letter from. I am completely alone. In my studies, I lag behind people the same age as me. Everybody attends *gimnazjum* [high school], but I am still in Grade 4. I will certainly not be able to achieve much. In general, my life is not as I imagined it would be.

My greatest dream is to find someone from my family or some relatives, or a stranger who could give me advice, tell me what to do, how to act, so that I would not always have to be alone because by myself I still do not know what to do or how to act. I need one living soul who can talk with me and give me advice.

I believe that my greatest act of heroism was during the deportation when I hid my mother. Instead of hiding myself, I forced my mother into the hiding place. Also when I found a way to escape

---

Shtibel, *The Violin*, page 118 of this volume.

from the gathering place and the Germans, and when I did not even turn around when the German called me. And later, when the police caught me and put me in jail and I got out through the window without anybody helping me. In general my whole life has been an act of heroism.

Poems

Poems by Rachel and Adam Shtibel's granddaughters.

WHY REMEMBER?

Why remember those horrible nights?
Why remember those frightening sights?
I don't think I want to remember
The emotions that flow so tender.
Remembering how all the Jews lost what they had.
Remembering the death of six million is sad.
I think I just want to forget.
That just might be my best bet yet.
But maybe I really should remember.
Maybe that's what is really better.
If everyone forgot it might happen once more.
And to freedom we might as well close our door.
Why remember those horrible nights?
Why remember those frightening sights?
I'll tell you why to do all those things,
To think of all the memories it brings.
To remember our friends and family lost,
But most of all, remember the horrors of the Holocaust.

Shari Zimmerman, 1994 (12 years old)

MEMORIES OF WAR

When I think of all the wars we had
My eyes begin to tear.
How could soldiers be so brave
When I feel so much fear.
I think of long and lonely days
And nights that were dark and cold.
How those soldiers had to fight
To save the young and old.
I hope I never have to see
Another tragic war,
Or feel the pain of loved ones lost
Gone forever more.
Today I wish for peace to come
To live in harmony,
To never have to cry again
To never know uncertainty.

Julie Zimmerman, 1994 (12 years old)

Glossary

bar mitzvah: [Hebrew: "one to whom the commandments apply"] The age of thirteen when, according to Jewish tradition, boys becomes religiously and morally responsible for their actions and are considered adults for the purpose of synagogue ritual; also, a synagogue ceremony marking attainment of this status, with the boy called upon to read the Torah publicly.

bubbie: [Yiddish; also Bubba, Bubbe, Bubby, Bobbe, Bobe] Grandmother.

Chai: [Hebrew: "living"] The word *chai* is comprised of the Hebrew letters *chet* and *yod*, the eighth and tenth letters of the alphabet, and corresponds to the numerical value of 18, which, according to Jewish tradition, makes eighteen a lucky number; symbol made up of the two Hebrew letters sometimes worn as a jewellery pendant and considered a good luck charm; *chai* and derivatives thereof (Chaim, Chaya) sometimes given as a name to Jewish children.

challah: [Hebrew] Braided egg bread traditionally eaten on Shabbat and other Jewish holidays.

chullent: [Yiddish; also *cholent*, *tcholent*] Slow-cooked pot stew often made for Shabbat by Jews of Eastern European descent; usually the main course of the festive Shabbat lunch served on Saturdays after the synagogue service.

cohen: [Hebrew: "priest"; also *kohen*] People who trace their ancestry to the priestly family of the biblical Aaron, brother of Moses, and who occupy a special ritual status within Judaism (such as reciting certain blessing in synagogues). According to Jewish tradition, particular rules apply to a *cohen,* such as having no contact with dead bodies and not marrying a divorcee or a convert to Judaism.

Gestapo: [German: short for *Geheime Staatspolizei*] The political police of Nazi Germany who ruthlessly and violently eliminated opposition to the Nazis within Germany and its occupied territories; responsible for the roundup of Jews throughout Europe for deportation to death camps; also, through its special "task force," the Einsatzgruppen, responsible for the roundup and murder of Jews in eastern Poland and the USSR in mass shooting operations.

Gypsies: Common term for the Sinti and Roma, a nomadic people who speak Romany, an Indo-European language. Like the Jews, they were identified by the Nazis as an inferior race and targeted for genocide; by war's end, between 250,000 and 500,000 had fallen victim to the Nazi genocide.

Hashomer Hatzair: [Hebrew: "The Young Guard"] Left-wing Zionist youth organization especially active in east-central Europe before and immediately after World War II; members and former members viewed with suspicion by Soviet-allied governments in the post-war period.

Hutzuls: [also Hutsuls, Gutzuls, Gutsuls] Small ethno-cultural group of highlanders who live in the northern areas of the Carpathian mountains.

kheyder: [Yiddish; also *cheder*] Elementary Hebrew school; traditionally attended by boys from the age of three.

kashruth: *See* kosher.

Kiddush: [Hebrew: "sanctification"] Blessing over wine recited on Shabbat and other Jewish holidays.

kilim: A colourful woven carpet or rug.

kolkhoz: [Russian: "collective farm"; short for *kollektivnoe khozyaistvo*] a cooperative agricultural enterprise operated on state-owned land, the *kolkhoz* was the dominant form of agricultural enterprise in the former Soviet Union.

kosher: [Hebrew: "fit to eat according to Jewish dietary laws"] Observant Jews follow a system of rules known as *kashruth* that regulates what can be eaten, how food is prepared, and how meat and poultry are slaughtered; food is kosher when it is deemed fit for consumption according to Jewish dietary laws; see also *shoykhet*.

minyen: [Hebrew; also *minyan*] The quorum of ten adult Jews required for prayer services; sometimes used as a synonym for a prayer group or service.

mitzvah: [Hebrew: "commanded deed"] Fundamental Jewish concept about the obligation of Jews to perform the commandments set forth in the Torah; often used to mean "good deed" or "act of kindness."

Passover: A spring festival marking the exodus of the Israelites from Egypt and their liberation from slavery, an event commemorated by the seder, a ritual feast where the story is recounted, and by the eating of unleavened bread (matzah).

Pidyon HaBen: (Hebrew: "Redemption of the Son"] Jewish ritual performed one month after birth of the firstborn son, where parents symbolically redeem their infant from a *cohen* (descendant of the ancient priests); based on a biblical concept of firstborn males as belonging to God.

Rosh Hashanah: [Hebrew: "New Year"] Autumn holiday that marks the beginning of the Jewish year.

Shabbat: [Hebrew: "Sabbath"; also *Shabbes, Shabbos*] Weekly day of rest beginning Friday at sunset and ending Saturday at nightfall; ushered in by the lighting of candles on Friday night and the recitation of blessings over wine and challah; a day of celebration as well as prayer, it is customary to eat three festive meals, attend synagogue services and refrain from doing any work or travel.

shoykhet: [Hebrew: "ritual slaughterer"; also *shochet*] Man conversant with the religious teachings of *kashruth*, trained to slaughter animals painlessly and check the meat afterward to be sure it is kosher; *see also* kosher.

sołtys: [Polish] Chairman of a village council.

Star of David: [in Hebrew: *Magen David*] Six-pointed star that is the ancient and most recognizable symbol of Judaism. During World War II, Jews in Nazi-occupied areas were frequently forced to wear a badge or armband with the Star of David on it as an identifying mark of their lesser status and to single them out as targets for persecution.

sukkah: [Hebrew: "hut"] Temporary shelter erected for the holiday of Sukkoth; traditionally decorated with plants and fruits and constructed with only a partial roof so that stars can be seen at night.

Sukkoth: [Hebrew: "Feast of Tabernacles"; also Sukkot] Autumn harvest festival recalling the forty years during which the ancient Israelites wandered the desert after their exodus from slavery in Egypt; lasting seven days, Jews traditionally eat meals during the holiday in a sukkah.

Torah: [Hebrew] The most important document in Judaism, Torah can be translated as either the "teaching" or the "law" and usually refers to the first five books of the Hebrew Bible (also called the Pentateuch); sometimes refers to the entire body of writing contained in what Christians call the Old Testament; sometimes used to denote the entire spectrum of authoritative Jewish written and oral religious teachings.

wójt: [Polish] Elected mayor of a rural commune – that is, one consisting only of villages.

Yom Kippur: [Hebrew: "Day of Atonement"] Holiest day of the Jewish calendar observed by fasting, prayer and repentance; occurs in the autumn, ten days after Rosh Hashanah.

zeyde: [Yiddish; also zeide] Grandfather.

Photographs

1 Sara and Israel Milbauer, 1929.
2 Rachel, 1936 (photo found in Velvel's violin case).
3 Velvel, wearing the embroidered shirt he often wore for his violin concerts, undated (photo found in Velvel's violin case).

1 Rachel with Sara Milbauer, 1935 (photo found in Velvel's violin case).
2 Rachel's aunt, Mina Blaufeld (right), Rachel at five years old (back, middle) and
   Aunt Mina's cousins, undated (photo found in Velvel's violin case).
3 Nelly (left), and Velvel's cousin Minka (right), undated. Rachel's only photo of
   Nelly (photo found in Velvel's violin case).

1 Rachel's grandmother, Judith Blaufeld (Bubbie Yetta), with Rachel in the garden
   in Turka, undated (photo found in Velvel's violin case).
2 Rachel with the ruins of Wrocław in the background, 1951.
3 Recent photo of Velvel's beloved violin resting on the kilim rug he made himself
   before the war. Both survived the war buried on the family farm in Turka.

1 & 2 Rachel playing the violin and at the piano, 1949.

3 Rachel, back left, playing with her violin troupe in Wrocław, 1948.

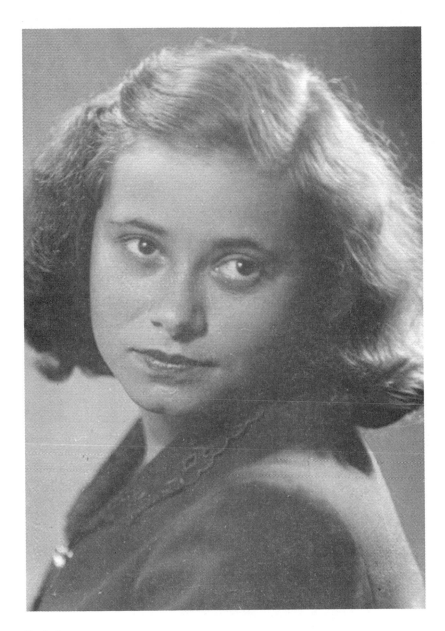

Rachel, 1955.

Adam's parents, Chaim and Basia Sztybel (standing), and grandmother, Esther (seated), before the war, undated.

1 Adam (far right), at the home for orphans in Warsaw, 1948.
2 Adam in the Polish air force. Deblin, Poland, 1950.
3 Adam in the Polish air force, 1952.

Adam, 1955.

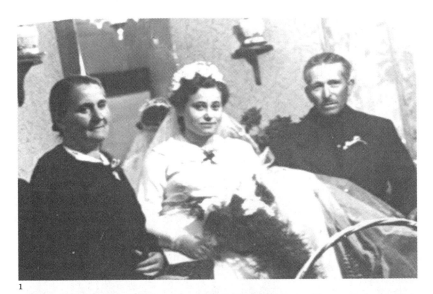

1

2

1   Rachel at her wedding, standing between Rozalia and Jozef Beck, the Polish couple who helped save her family, 1956.

2   Rachel and Adam's wedding photo, 1956.

1   Adam in the Israel Defense Forces, 1967.
2   Rachel working in her lab in Rehovot, Israel, undated.
3   Adam and Rachel in Israel, 1967.
4   Rachel and Adam's fiftieth wedding anniversary, 2006.

Index · The Violin

Index · A Child's Testimony

The Azrieli Foundation was established in 1989 to realize and extend the philanthropic vision of David J. Azrieli, C.M., C.Q., M.Arch. The Foundation's mission is to support a wide spectrum of initiatives in education and research. The Azrieli Foundation is an active supporter of programs in the fields of Education, the education of architects, scientific and medical research, and the arts. The Azrieli Foundation's many initiatives include: the Holocaust Survivor Memoirs Program, which collects, preserves, publishes and distributes the written memoirs of survivors in Canada; the Azrieli Institute for Educational Empowerment, an innovative program successfully working to keep at-risk youth in school; the Azrieli Fellows Program, which promotes academic excellence and leadership on the graduate level at Israeli universities; the Azrieli Music Project, which celebrates and fosters the creation of high-quality new Jewish orchestral music; and the Azrieli Neurodevelopmental Research Program, which supports advanced research on neurodevelopmental disorders, particularly Fragile X and Autism Spectrum Disorders.